THE MINER
SPECIAL ISSUE
JOURNAL OF THE NATIONAL UNION OF MINEWORKERS

FRIDAY, JUNE 15th, 1984

STOP PRESS
Talks collapse
Talks broken off and Coal Board negotiating position in chaos as *The Miner* went to Press. Chairman Ian MacGregor's wild claims on situation in the industry earlier contradicted by other high-ranking Coal Board members.

With NUM standing 100 per cent behind its position that pit closure list be withdrawn, Coal Board chaos expected to grow in the weeks ahead as summer ebbs away.

Meanwhile increased support from the rail, sea and transport unions was choking off fuel supplies as the NUM's NEC met to discuss the rapidly escalating situation.

GOTCHA!

Troops drive police van in miners' demonstration

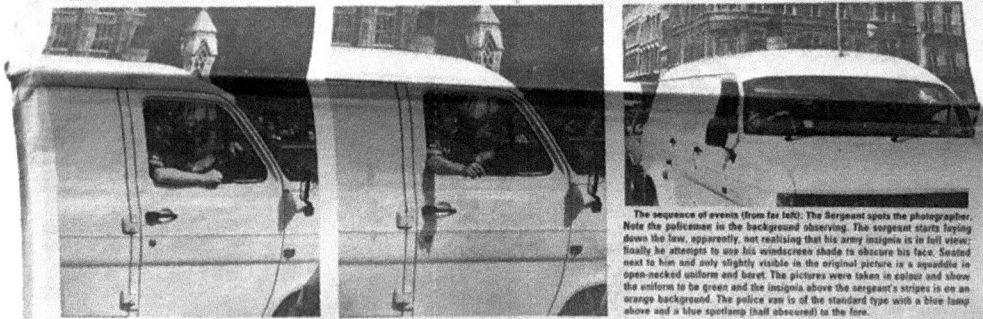

The sequence of events (from far left): The Sergeant spots the photographer. Note the policeman in the background observing. The sergeant starts laying down the law, apparently, not realising that his army insignia is in full view; finally he attempts to use his windscreen shade to obscure his face. Seated next to him and only slightly visible in the original picture is a squaddie in open-necked uniform and beret. The pictures were taken in colour and show the uniform to be green and the insignia above the sergeant's stripes is on an orange background. The police van is of the standard type with a blue lamp above and a blue spotlamp (half obscured) to the fore.

The Government IS using troops in the miners' strike.

Photographic evidence of military involvement has been obtained by *The Miner.*

The sensational evidence contradicts absolutely Government claims that there has been no such involvement.

Coming on top of recent douments revealing major political interference in the strike — something always denied by the Government — an almighty row is sure to follow.

The photos, taken at the miners' mass lobby of Parliament on June 7th, show an Army sergeant driving a police van. The vehicle was one of many swiftly deployed as the size of the demonstration rapidly grew.

Yorkshire miner Tony Lowe, a keen amateur photographer, spotted the sergeant driving the van towards Parliament Square and immediately began clicking away.

EXPOSED FILM

Realising what was happening, the sergeant tried to hide behind his specially darkened windscreen, and obscure his face. But Tony had already snatched enough shots.

The sergeant then yelled at police nearby "nick that bastard . . . get the camera." There followed a series of amazing scenes in the heart of the capital city.

Tony, knowing that the film would be lost if he were caught, dodged

EXCLUSIVE
By The Editor

between two vans as the police gave chase. It gained him a few precious seconds to wind the film on.

He carried on running, got among a group of other miners and threw the film to one, shouting to him to guard it with his life.

With the police breathing down his neck he told the other miners to surround him as he feverishly put another film in the camera.

A fight between one of the miners and a chasing policeman gave Tony a few more seconds before the police got to him.

In full view of the public and at least four named NUM witnesses, the police demanded the camera, opened the back and exposed the film to the light.

Only now will they be aware that they got the wrong film.

Time after time, the Government has denied that troops are involved in the strike, despite a continuing flood of disturbing reports.

These pictures show that the Government has yet again been lying through its teeth.

Political embarrassment will now be acute and credibility reduced to a new low.

▲ *The Miner* reports on military involvement in policing the strike

work/class/unions

Hilary Cave
Recollections of the Miners' Strike

Police in riot gear going over the top against miners

Scargill ple
eten nelic

▲ Overleaf: *The Morning Star* reports police violence at Orgreave

ve yesterday.   (Photo: Martin Jenkinson).

: help us
brutality

Published by Manifesto Press Cooperative 2024

ISBN **978-1-907464-62-1**

Typeset in Bodoni and Gill

Contents

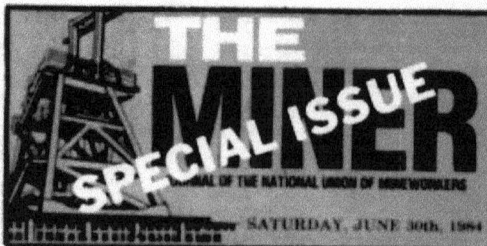

THE MINER

SPECIAL ISSUE

JOURNAL OF THE NATIONAL UNION OF MINEWORKERS

SATURDAY, JUNE 30th, 1984

STOP PRESS

Talks between NUM and steel union ISTC ended witho agreement on June 29th. Moves meanwhile going ahead tighten blockade and to ensure no steel production. Talks w rail and other transport unions planned to step up action. NU emphasised at talks that it was in everybody's interests increase the action. For if British coal industry was cut back would pave the way for reduced coal traffic by rail and lead further cuts in British Steel.

Ian MacGregor, who remains a member of the Board British Steel, believed to be actively involved behind the scene

TIME IS NOW ON OUR SIDE

By NUM President ARTHUR SCARGILL

The strike pendulum has now securely swung to our territory.

The most crucial date in the calendar — June 21st, the Longest Day — is passed. From here on in, the days get shorter and the nights longer.

We shall be entering autumn in an immensely *powerful* position with coal stocks at approximately 15m tonnes — well below the 17m tonne level at which the three-day week was introduced 10 years ago.

No Government — no matter which lunatic runs it — can go into the autumn in such a position. It would be a recipe for the most widespread industrial chaos ever witnessed.

And that is why I repeat what I have said throughout this dispute. Stand firm, hold your nerve and we shall register the greatest and most far reaching industrial victory this century.

Absolutely no one can be in any doubt whatever as to what is at stake in this dispute.

MacGregor's statement to Derbyshire directors that he wants to try to smash the NUM indicates his mentality perfectly.

But he is living in a fantasy world.

All he has succeeded in doing is achieving greater levels of unity in the NEC, with the last meeting calling unanimously for his instant dismissal.

But we should never allow MacGregor or any other individual to cloud the essence of our fight.

That essence was brought home to me just a week ago in a special article in a Sunday newspaper.

The paper reported that in Liverpool there are now between 10,000 and 20,000 youngsters on heroin.

The hopelessness and helplessness of unemployment has reduced the flower of a city's youth to the devastating world of hard drugs.

Where once young people could look forward to their working lives with hope, now they are around them the human and physical waste, deliberately created as a matter of Government policy.

It is that which we are fighting against.

I believe there is no one who can stand aside from that fight in the mistaken belief that if they keep their heads down they will be treated more leniently by this Government.

That is why I say to the steelworkers in particular, join with us. Do no be misled

Titanic

Once the pits have been butchered, attention will once again be turned on your own industry, creating more dole queue fodder. And when that day dawns who will be left to fight together with you?

Before our strike you were already living a highly uncertain existence, not knowing whether your jobs would survive from one year the next.

The only way to end t uncertainty is to join w us in fighting for and se ring a sound, secure expanding industrial ba in Britain.

And that message c be extended to all grou throughout this countr.

The miners of Brit are involved in a tot struggle to turn the tide human suffering.

Our heroic young m and the magnifice wives are lighting beacon for all.

I urge everyone, you old, man and woman, e ployed and unemploy join with us and suppo us in whatever way w can

Together we shall the foundations for a cure and decent future which the reality of becomes worthwhile—r something to escape fr on the end of hypodermic syringe.

London pride

A 50,000 turn-out fo mass demonstration London crowned a hug effective Day of Actio the South East in supp of the strike.

Rail transport virtu ground to a halt, the national newspape failed to appear in south and the distribut and content of others w severely cut ba thousands of health wo ers, teachers, office a factory workers joined the action, making a ju jar impact across the given.

As the London dem stration passed throu Fleet Street it was par cularly noticeable h hundreds of print worke lined the pavements applaud the marche Many of the print men a deeply disgusted with t anti-miner, one sid coverage of the dispute.

Also evident was overwhelming degree public support in the gion. Collecting bucke were full to overflowing a short time as men a women, young and o showed their recognitic that the miners fig against mass unemploy ment and the run-dow Britain is their fight

NOW TELL US YOU DEFEND THE RULE OF LAW IN G.B.

A mounted policeman prepares to bring a truncheon crashing down on the unprotected head of a woman at Orgreave in a scene which could have come straight out of Nazi Germany. The woman's crime? She had called for help for a middle-aged injured miner.

But for the speedy response of another miner who charged Lesley Boulton to the ground, it is certain that she would have suffered serious head injuries.

The action of the miner enabled her to escape with just a scalp graze from the truncheon. Lesley would like the two miners involved to contact her. That contact can be made through *The Miner* by phoning the Editor on 0742 700388.

Meanwhile, this picture, and others on page 7, should alert the whole country to the sickening levels of police violence now in operation.

We ask that one question of the mounted policeman: Is this a picture he would be proud to show his wife and children?

1 Thatcher's Law

Arrest I am travelling with NUM chief executive Roger Windsor to Mansfield to meet a group of councillors and senior police officers so we can negotiate a reasonable route through the town for the NUM Miners' March on Mansfield next month. To see for ourselves what the police are up to in Nottinghamshire we decide to use minor roads rather than the M1, but as the far north of the county is unknown territory I am never sure exactly where we are when we meet the first roadblock. We join a queue of vehicles containing men, sometimes single, sometimes in groups, who are being spoken to by police and then turned back, one by one. When my turn for questioning arrives the policeman is aggressive.

"Where are you going?"

"We're going to Mansfield."

I speak in a determined voice because I'm not going to let him intimidate me.

"Where've you come from?"

"Sheffield."

"Well, you're going to turn round and go back there. I can see you're pickets."

That damned badge of Roger's! At the start of the strike he ordered a supply of fancy, brightly coloured cardboard badges that announce the wearer as a Marshal. The rest of us, thinking they are silly, have nicknamed them sheriff's badges – but not in Roger's hearing. Why on earth is he wearing it today?

"No, we're not pickets. We have to get to a meeting in Mansfield."

"No, you don't" he orders. "You're going to turn round and go back to Sheffield."

"We have to get to Mansfield for a meeting – I'm not turning round."

He beckons another policeman who walks towards us, truncheon drawn and raised, as though a woman and a man sitting in a car pose some sort of threat to them. They certainly feel threatening to me. I know a Derbyshire miner whose windscreen was smashed by a policeman just last week as he sat in his car, so feel convinced that's what will happen to us. Suddenly it's like watching a hackneyed film, with everything seeming to move in slow motion. Trying not to let my fear show, I tell myself to close my eyes to protect my sight once the windscreen glass starts to shower over us. There is no chance of escape, as the first police officer is holding onto my car door. Anyway, trying to escape might suggest we've done something wrong. Hours seem to pass before the second policeman reaches the front of my car, but despite my fears he doesn't use his truncheon to smash the glass in our faces. I am still trying to get used to this unexpected turn of events when the first policeman resumes his threats to me as the driver.

"You're going to turn round and go back or I'll arrest you."

We have to reach this morning's meeting or we won't be able to hold the march and rally in Mansfield next month.

"Carry on, arrest me: we've done nothing wrong, and we're going to Mansfield for a meeting".

Now I have already learned, in the few weeks since the start of the strike, that absence of wrongdoing provides neither physical nor legal defence against the police, so I don't expect my claim of innocence to carry any weight with this copper. As anticipated, he begins to intone the words of an arrest, including the required caution. All I can do is wait for him to finish arresting me, then cope with whatever follows. Yet partway through the process his voice falters then stops for no apparent reason. I begin to realise this is how he is forcing the other drivers to turn back: he is threatening to arrest them. No-one before me seems to have resisted right up until the point of arrest, so my continuing refusal to back down appears to mystify this officer. After an awkward pause he simply abandons the arrest, speaks into his walkie-talkie and tells those at the next roadblock along the road to let my car through.

Our meeting will be tricky as we suspect all the Mansfield district councillors are working miners. They will be unhappy with our proposal to assemble thousands of our striking members to march through their town in what we are calling Miners March on Mansfield. We have already found that the police treat us as enemies, yet we need to negotiate permission to march from both councillors and police, as well as agreement on a reasonable route. Because the police roadblock has taken up more time than expected, we are late for the meeting. Walking into the meeting room at Mansfield Council Offices, Roger announces breezily

"Sorry we're late, but Hilary got arrested on the way here."

Suddenly the room feels electric, with someone asking

"What happened?"

"The police officer told me I had to turn round and go back to Sheffield, but I insisted that we had to come to Mansfield for a meeting."

As nobody offers any comment on that, we carry on with the meeting, trying to be patient and polite despite our inner feelings. Eventually we win grudging acceptance of a reasonable route for our march. As we are about to leave we are approached by the police representative, resplendent in pips and metallic braid, who introduced himself to the meeting as head of operations for Nottinghamshire Police. He is clearly unhappy.

"Did you tell my officers you were coming to meet me?"

"No, we shouldn't have needed to."

"All we did was tell the truth, that we had to attend a meeting in Mansfield. That should have been enough".

This goes down very badly.

"I know when my officers are being set up!"

He marches away, clearly feeling his dignity restored now he has uncovered our alleged plot.

That senior police officer was simply one small moving part in the machine of Thatcher's Law, the increasingly intrusive use of every lever of state power to defeat the National Union of Mineworkers and weaken the entire trade union movement. Yet prime minister Margaret Thatcher did not dream up these ideas up on her own: instead she followed the script of the play already written in the Ridley Report.

2 Facework: Pit visits

Thurcroft   All NUM National Office staff were expected to make underground visits to collieries so we could understand the working conditions of our members. My first pit visit, made with a group of office staff, was to Thurcroft near Rotherham. We had not been underground long before we came to a hot, dusty place where men were shovelling. All we could do was watch, but I was not used to standing idle while other people worked, so I felt uncomfortable. After a while one of the miners straightened his back painfully then looked around at this group of women watching him work. We'd not been underground long and must still have had clean faces. Clearly fed up, he walked up to me then wiped his hand, black with coal dust and muck, slowly and deliberately twice across my face. I just stood there and let him, knowing that in his shoes I would have wanted to do the same. Later we arrived at a coal face that was lit by electric lights. In my innocence I said what an improvement that must be, but I was puzzled because none of the miners there seemed to agree. When I'd pressed the point a bit more one of the men told me

"Well, if you've only got light from our own cap lamps you can find a quiet spot and have a sleep if you're tired, but you can't do that if it's all lit up. If Deputy catches you asleep, it's the sack."

Light finally dawned in my dim brain about why a lit-up coal face was not popular.

After the general office visit underground, senior staff took it in turns to join Arthur Scargill on his regular pit visits in England, Scotland and Wales. It was sobering to see the conditions in which miners had to work, as well as to realise how little was provided for them underground. There were no toilets, no hot food or drink, no running water supplies. Miners had to carry every morsel of food and liquid underground themselves. Trevor Cave, who had visited coalfields in the Soviet Union, said that miners there were provided with hot food underground, but in Britain that was said to be impossible because of the fire danger from electricity. That claim did not explain how electrically-powered machinery could be operated safely underground to produce coal but not to provide hot food.

Markham   On one of my underground visits with Arthur Scargill we went to Markham, just outside Chesterfield, where I already knew some of the NUM officials showing us round. Markham had been the site of a disaster in 1973 when mechanical failure had caused a cage carrying miners underground to fall down the shaft, smashing into the bottom at great speed. Eighteen men had died, with twelve more very seriously injured. For the past ten years I had known the disaster had traumatised many more miners because in 1973 I had worked in the Surveyor's department of Clay Cross Council, where I saw, week after week, miners coming in to plead for jobs because they couldn't face riding down in the cage after that terrible event. As our cage dropped down the Markham pit shaft I tried not to think about the disaster. Could the Markham miners who descended in the cage for each daily shift ever forget the disaster, or did they force forgetfulness on themselves as the only possible way of steeling themselves to step into that cage?

Every visit by Arthur Scargill, their union President, was seen as an occasion by our members, as it gave them the opportunity to speak to him directly. Underground at Markham that day, we were walking along a roadway. Now let's not get too impressed by the term "roadway", as all it meant was hard-packed earth with lots of items sticking up that might cause us to trip. A miner came up to Arthur Scargill and asked "Why are you always so militant, Arthur?"

Arthur immediately sat down in the roadway, followed by the miner. Then he started to answer the question patiently while our member followed intently. As it took a while I realised, listening in, that relating to his members was what Arthur did best.

Durham and Eppleton   Another pit visit I made on our Scargill-accompanying roster was to Eppleton in County Durham. Our first stop was in the city at Redhills, home to the NUM's Durham Area. A palatial building set in its own grounds, Redhills was a reminder of the huge numbers of men who had worked the Durham coalfield. It was also the home of the Durham Area General Secretary, so that he could be reached immediately in case of any emergency. After a friendly cup of tea with Tommy Callan, the courteous, gently-spoken General Secretary of that time, we took our bags to the hotel. NUM officials always stayed at the Royal County, the best hotel in Durham. Its many comforts, including chocolates in the room, provided a real contrast to my modest lifestyle.

Tommy and his wife joined us for a meal at the hotel. While the cheeseboard was being offered, she asked Arthur what his favourite cheese was?

"Oh, it's Wensleydale – I'm a Yorkshire lad."

As there was no Wensleydale on the board, she summoned the waiter and asked if they had any.

"I'm very sorry, madam, we don't have any." Picking up her displeasure, he tried to oblige. "If you like I could send round to The Three Tuns and try to get some from there."

Arthur was clearly regretting having answered Mrs Callan's question honestly.

"There's no need, thanks, I'm perfectly happy with what's already here."

Our hostess was adamant, though: "You're our guest here in Durham, so we must make you as comfortable as possible."

She asked the waiter to do what he could, so very quickly a wedge of Wensleydale arrived from the second-best hotel in Durham, just around the corner. That was how things were in the NUM before the strike: the National President, whoever he might be, was regarded as an honoured guest in every coalfield he visited.

Next morning we drove to Eppleton, a very old colliery, where Arthur and his driver Jim went into the miners' communal changing room. I was shown into the medical room to change. The medical attendant, keen to help, offered me a triangular bandage to keep my long hair clean when we went underground.

Outside, struggling to get my knee pads on, I realised what a rare species women were in a pit yard. Suddenly several men were gathered round trying to help, although as there were only two buckles to be fastened behind each knee, and as I only had two legs, there wasn't really room enough for all the would-be helpers. Walking across the pit yard in a regulation boiler suit and heavy pit boots felt odd enough, but once we had strapped on our self-rescuers and batteries for our lamps I felt really weighed down. How did miners do hard physical work while carrying all this lot around?

In order to get underground we had to crowd into the cage. Although it was in theory a lift, the cage felt more like an animal cage than anything else. As usual, I hid my unease about the descent.

Once we had reached the pit bottom we started to walk towards the face. What struck me about Eppleton was the atmosphere. In that old pit I somehow felt the passing shadows of previous generations of miners – a very strange sensation. There were more pressing matters to deal with, though.

"Now, Arthur, we're going up there on the manrider." This, a conveyor belt that was always moving, could save a lot of time and effort. Our guide turned to me.

"It's far too dangerous for a woman, Hilary, so you'll need to walk up that slope. Bert'll take you up there, and we'll meet you at the top." Following his gaze, I could see that the slope was very steep and long. Why should I have to climb all the way up there, hampered by knee pads, helmet and lamp, battery and self-rescuer strapped round my waist, when the men were going to ride up on the belt?

Letting Mrs Callan's public reverence for the union's National President be my guide, I spoke firmly.

"If it's safe enough for the President, it's safe enough for me. I'll go on the manrider with the rest of you." There was an uncomfortable silence, but as they sensed I wasn't going to back down, we all got onto the belt for the ascent. Climbing onto the manrider was hardly an inviting prospect, but apart from the difficulty of getting on and off, it was going to be much easier than slogging up a long incline. As the belt never stopped moving I braced myself mentally then stepped on as carefully and quickly as possible. Dithering at that point could have caused a fall. Once on the belt we had to move quickly, kneeling down then stretching flat onto our bellies. When it was nearly time to leave it, we had to reverse that process in order to stand up again, then judge the right moment to step off.

Once we had ridden back to the surface in the cage I went into the medical centre to get clean and dressed. I felt filthy. After the darkness underground the light and airy medical room was very welcome. Touched to see that the attendant had already filled the bath I thanked him for his kindness.

"Well, I always run a bath for the lads if they come up injured."

As the triangular bandage hadn't kept the coal dust out of my long hair I had to wash and dry it. Twice the attendant knocked on the door and said

"Arthur's sent to see if you're ready yet." As I'd just broken my hairbrush in the tangles, I thought how typical of him to be in such a hurry, but did my best to speed up.

Once the pit visit was over I was tired, so felt glad to rest in the car as Jim drove us away. That quiet time gave me chance to reflect on the tremendous physical demands made on the Coal Board's underground workers. It would have been sensible for management to consider miners' health when designing equipment, but this never seemed to have occurred to them. During each underground visit, I found that mechanisms for moving us about seemed to have been designed to be as uncomfortable as possible. The cages that took us underground always seemed to have entrances that were too low to step into without bending our heads. Paddy wagons, a type of underground transport that would take us to distant faces, had as their backrests one thin metal rod that ran horizontally across the human back in what felt like the worst possible place. If it felt very uncomfortable to me, although I had never had a do a minute's work underground, imagine what it was like to sit back onto that when you'd spent a full shift underground doing physical work. For the length of their shift, miners only had the hard-packed mucky earth of the pit bottom to rest on while they ate a bit of food in their break. I never expected luxury underground, but surely miners would have benefited if metal backrests on paddy wagons had supported their backs rather than digging into the spine and muscles. It would surely have helped reduce the number of absences caused by bad backs. Would it have been too much to ask for cage entry gates to have been just a little higher, so miners could step in and out without stooping and risking jarring their necks?

After the pit visit Jim drove us to a Miners' Welfare where Arthur was to address a union meeting. Welfares were social clubs providing for the whole community. Part-financed by mandatory weekly payments from miners' wages, they provided space for everything from children's Christmas parties to NUM branch meetings to fishing clubs. Sitting on stage behind Arthur, I could sense an atmosphere very different from the goodwill we'd met earlier that day down the pit. The room was full of angry faces.

During this period the overtime ban, agreed at Special Delegate Conference the previous October, had been making serious inroads into the wages of the craftsmen (fitters and electricians) who normally made most of their money doing maintenance work on weekend overtime shifts. That enabled production to re-start immediately once miners arrived underground on the first Monday shift. The overtime ban had two purposes. Firstly it was intended to pressure the Coal Board because they had refused to settle our outstanding pay claim. Secondly it would reduce coal stocks before the looming showdown over pit closures and job losses. As the meeting got under way in the Welfare our members were muttering and calling out to express their frustration. I could see and feel that this was going to be a difficult meeting. Could Arthur win over these restive members who had already lost a lot of money? I needn't have worried. His usual mix of organised facts, reasoned eloquence and humour flowed out across the hall. As the meeting went on I could feel the tension evaporating. He was applauded warmly at the end. How had he turned that meeting around? I had watched and listened, but still didn't quite know how the magic had been worked.

The rest of the evening was more relaxed as we all mingled, chatted and had a drink. Someone brought up a man who was introduced as the local MP. I will call him Joe Bloggs. As he spoke, memory began to stir. His name had been adjusted slightly, he had put on weight, but surely it was the same person I had known fifteen years before.

"Didn't we know each other on Teesside?" I asked, looking hard at Joe to check my impression. Suddenly he seemed very uncomfortable. We had been members of the same political group in the past, when his work involved young people. He had angered a couple of us by encouraging some of these under-age youngsters to smoke cannabis and drink alcohol with him. We had feared his behaviour, if uncovered, might bring our group into disrepute, as well as wrecking his career. Joe's eyes began to register alarm as he realised that here was someone from his past who could, even now, damage his political career. He excused himself quickly, hurrying away and spending the rest of the evening talking to people at the far end of the room. Privately I found his behaviour amusing. Why did he think I would want to harm him by speaking to anyone else about what he had done as a younger man? Of course I made no mention to Arthur and Jim of what I knew about that local MP.

Comrie My next pit visit was to Comrie in Scotland. NUM Scottish Area President Mick McGahey had a chronically bad chest, so he was unfit to go underground. His deputy George Bolton acted as our guide instead. As soon as they saw a group of miners using shovels underground, Arthur and Jim were alarmed. One of them muttered "they're hand-filling..." while the other murmured "there's been no investment in this pit – that means they're intending to shut it." At Comrie I came nearest to having an accident underground. Heading towards the cage that would lift us to the surface, we were on a manrider that was moving at frightening speed, then we had got to our feet ready to jump off. It all felt wrong: somehow I knew my balance wasn't right but if I hesitated any longer the belt would have taken me past the jumping-off platform. I jumped but knew I was misjudging it. Then I found myself falling forward, off the platform. Luckily George Bolton had spotted the danger so he stepped forward and caught me, for which I was very grateful. Now George and I were not friends. Outside work, we knew each other in our political lives, usually finding ourselves on opposing sides of an argument. If I'd had to choose the person who would save me from an accident, I would not have chosen George, nor would he have chosen me as the person to save from a nasty fall. We were underground, though, so he did what miners always do: he acted quickly to protect another person from harm. That same manrider seemed hazardous: on a later visit my colleague Dave Feickert had a problem getting off it in that same place. Unfortunately no-one was able to catch him, so as he fell he cut his head open. Those visits showed us, as staff members, how hard and dangerous underground work could be.

An evening rally followed our underground visit to Comrie. Sitting on the high veranda that ran round three sides of a building like a nonconformist church hall, I was listening to Mick McGahey, then Arthur Scargill, speak. Those two had apparently agreed that McGahey would call on Scottish miners to strike but Mick failed to make that call so Arthur I felt obliged to do so instead. Afterwards Mick said he had forgotten to call for the strike, which seemed an odd lapse of memory in the circumstances. Anyway, Scottish miners took strike action in time to seek and win approval at the March 1984 NEC meeting. That visit to Comrie was my last underground trip because pit visits ended as soon as the strike began. So far as I could tell, they never resumed, so I believed the Coal Board had told Arthur he would no longer be welcome underground.

3 Thatcher's Law Two

The Ridley Report During the 1970's trades unions had often been strong, although that did not necessarily mean that their members lived in comfort. The National Union of Mineworkers (NUM), whose members had slipped far down the earnings league over a long period, had been able to win pay rises by strike action in 1972 and 1974. But strong trades unions did not suit everyone, including many of those with powerful connections and the expectation of coming into government. Even before their 1979 General Election victory the Tories began to plan for change. The Selsdon Group of ultra-right Tory MPs produced the Ridley Report, named after its main author. Nicholas Ridley came from a mine-owning family whose great wealth had literally been made on the backs of miners in North East England. That Report set out a plan to wreck the power of trades unions in a nationalised industry, so preparing it for privatisation. It was expected that once the rock face had been broken open by a single privatisation, the remaining nationalised industries would crumble through the gap. Following a leak, The *Economist* journal published part of the report, sometimes termed the Ridley Plan, late in the 1970's. The Report named several possible nationalised industries as targets of such a transformation. Like a serious geological fault in a colliery, the Ridley Plan had the potential to destroy the viability of all nationalised industries, but this seismic potential, created deliberately by politicians, was entirely avoidable.

The prior existence and use by Government of the Ridley Plan shows that the miners' strike was not merely a personality clash between Margaret Thatcher and Arthur Scargill, which is often claimed. All major moves had been mapped out by the Selsdon Group before the Tories were elected. Once Margaret Thatcher became Prime Minister in 1979 her Government used its powers to make changes that would turn the Plan into reality. Social security rules were altered to penalise strikers and their families. Other levers of state power were also used by Government, which commissioned a report about the coal industry to be undertaken by the Monopolies and Mergers Commission. Government also set about manipulating markets for coal and other power industries in a way that disadvantaged coal. A series of new laws, starting with the 1980 Employment Act, made it harder for unions to operate effectively. Policing was transformed: it had previously been managed locally, by Chief Police Officers wielding autocratic powers. In 1984 policing became in effect a centralised national body, used by Government as a weapon against our union and its members, who were merely trying to save their industry. The Ridley Plan had stated that police needed to be trained in riot techniques. Civil and criminal law were used against us, while newspapers and broadcasting media joined enthusiastically in those attacks. We will look later at the effects of all those changes.

4 The Lamp Cabin One

Most people think of miners' lamps as the old-fashioned kind with a real flame, carried by hand. Although those were used by some miners, underground workers who needed to move about carried much less romantic lamps. With a bulb and reflector slotted into a groove on the helmet, each lamp was attached by cable to a heavy battery carried on the belt. Between shifts that equipment was placed on charge in the lamp cabin.

To me, the education and campaigning work undertaken by the NUM was like the lamp cabin because it charged up our members' ability to see, and then to understand, what was happening to their union and industry. They were then better-prepared to take action at work and to take part in decisions about what the union should do.

Having been appointed as NUM National Education Officer from May 1983, I was responsible for organising national opportunities for learning. When I started to look at how NUM education had been organised, I was dismayed to find that attendance at the national residential courses, called schools, had been seen almost as rewards for long service. Areas seemed to nominate long-serving union members who were close to retirement, while the courses were often held at seaside hotels. I had spent several years teaching on TUC shop stewards' courses, where we had used lots of group work to encourage active participation rather than passive listening. Today that is considered standard practice, but had not been so in the 1980's. That experience made me determined to change the NUM's approach to education. It needed, I thought, to link active learning, knowledge and consideration of the problems facing our union, its members and the industry. That would be the most effective basis for action. I wanted to arrange future national schools in coalfield venues such as Northern College, a new radical college in South Yorkshire for second-chance learning for adults; or Wortley Hall, which was closely connected to the labour movement.

Arthur Scargill approved that approach, as did Peter Heathfield once he took office in March 1984, so my letters to Area Secretaries began to encourage them to send younger activists to national NUM schools. Eric Eaton, working at Newstead colliery, recalls that he was encouraged by his Notts area to attend the March 1984 school focused on our *Campaign for Coal* materials "because they were looking for younger ones".

On joining the staff team I had quickly picked up a clearer understanding of the threat facing the coal industry. It was well known that Thatcher's government had previously advanced a plan for pit closures, only retreating in the face of determined opposition. No one in the union believed she would not fight back, but with better preparations. After all, the Ridley Report had set out a detailed plan for defeating a major trade union in a nationalised sector, so opening the door to privatisation. It was clear that the NUM needed to prepare for the coming storm.

Pit closures had been going on for a long time but had not previously been conducted with the callous enthusiasm that Iain MacGregor, the Coal Board's new Chairman, had shown towards cutting jobs in the British steel industry. He had also been a very senior manager at British Leyland when trades union convenor Derek Robinson had been victimised. Knowing that a quick response was needed to MacGregor's appointment, we devised a poster showing him as a butcher with a cleaver, bent on hacking up our industry. Frank Watters, who did valuable work behind the scenes for Arthur Scargill and the NUM, was involved in this project, liaising with our Doncaster printers. We were upset to discover that we (I think it was my mistake) had mis-spelled MacGregor's name. Frank shook his head mournfully, muttering in his strong Scots accent

"We got it wrong – he's a Scots bastard, not an Irish bastard!"

The poster had to be reprinted.

Of course we needed a full-scale campaign, not just a single poster, if we were to defend our industry and our union. Apart from campaigns within the union's branches and Areas, I was one of a staff team at National Office who, understanding the seriousness of the threat, were keen to work hard to save our union, our industry and our mining communities. Soon after I started work at the NUM, the idea of a Staff Campaign Committee seemed to come from Arthur Scargill's office. Senior staff gathered to discuss how we could best contribute to what we knew would be a massive effort. At the time I felt pleased to be elected as chairperson of this group, only afterwards beginning to wonder if I had been chosen simply because as a newcomer I was not yet overburdened with diary commitments. During our discussions we agreed that it would be important to give our members as much information as possible about what was at stake, so they would be able to argue our case effectively.

Nell Myers, Arthur's PA, pointed out in a briefing note that the support of coalfield women would be needed. She reminded us that miners' wives had sometimes been used to oppose and undermine industrial action by miners. We agreed that our campaign should be aimed at women as well as men, featuring the bad effects of pit closures on families and whole coalfield communities, not just on jobs that were mainly for men. Only many years afterwards did I discover that Jean McCrindle of Northern College had previously sent a message to Arthur Scargill, pointing out that some NUM officials in Yorkshire had previously discouraged coalfield women from attending campaign meetings, and that this had been very unhelpful. Presumably Arthur had forgotten that message, as he did not share it with me, nor apparently with Nell. As Yorkshire was the largest NUM Area, the lack of understanding amongst some leading people there was a serious weakness. Had we been aware of the problem we might have been able to convince them that women would be a vital resource in our coming battle.

Our staff campaign committee decided to produce folders of six, later seven, booklets for Area and branch officials, as well as for coalfield women and other members of coalfield communities. The campaign packs would deal with such topics as the economic and social costs of pit closures, new ways of using coal, the dangers of privatisation, misleading Coal Board accounting practices and Government policies that worked against the coal industry. Our Industrial Relations and Research Departments would produce texts for the detailed booklets. Those would be passed to me for editing into a shared house style. For those of our members who could not easily handle that amount of information, Maurice Jones, editor of our newspaper The Miner, convinced me that we needed cartoons to make key points as part of a short pamphlet. I would write the pamphlet, while Maurice would engage the cartoonist. Once all that material had been written, I had to arrange printing and distribution. Many thousands of copies were required for this extensive and expensive programme of publicity, and I thought at the time that it would reach deep into our membership and the coalfield communities.

Multiple copies of our *Campaign for Coal* packs were being sent to Area Offices, with a letter from me asking Area Secretaries to arrange for circulation to every branch, assuring them that there were enough copies for each branch committee member and activists. Those packs were dear to my heart because of all the months of work that had gone into their creation and production. I arranged advance delivery of some boxes of the packs to National Office so I could give one to each delegate at the October 1983 Special Conference. Despite my attachment to them, it was going to be a pain to get them to London for the Special Conference, so I needed to hire a taxi to get myself and the packs to the train. As I met up with the Derbyshire delegation on the train, they helped me at the other end.

What I did not know until several years later was that there seemed to be distribution problems in the Notts Area. One Saturday morning in 1986 I was standing in Hucknall market place with a number of local miners, campaigning against the abrupt closure of the town's Bottom Pit. Those miners had all been stalwart strikers who in Notts had proudly called themselves Loyal to the Last. They told me that when they had briefly occupied the Notts Area offices in Mansfield in 1984, they had found our *Campaign for Coal* briefing packs still in their cardboard boxes. Apparently they had never been circulated to branches, so the vast majority of the Notts miners had never been given the chance to see our detailed arguments about why we needed to defend the coal industry. Had this been a mistake made by Area Secretary Henry Richardson, not long in post, or had there been some interference by other officials or staff members? I have never been able to find out. The problem may also have been more localised, as miners at one pit in South Notts recalled that their branch secretary was fond of binning material that might create a lot of work for him. There has always been a question about why so few Notts miners supported the strike. Could part of the answer be that they were never made aware of all the arguments for protecting the industry and its jobs from the onslaught of the Tory Government, which was being driven by what we would today call neoliberal ideology?

Other NUM Areas, where the briefing packs were circulated, had much better responses to the strike call made by Special Delegate Conference later, in April 1984. Activist Steve Brunt of Arkwright recalled that Derbyshire made extensive use of those campaign packs, and that he still had his pack at home, forty years on. Another Area which valued that campaign material was Durham Mechanics. They asked me to arrange a day school, based around the packs, to train up their activists. Anne Suddick, PA to Area Secretary Bill Etherington, impressed me by her organising ability and commitment. I had explained that we needed to sort out small groups who could work together at various points during the day. Knowing every one of the participants, she had made rapid assessments: A and B would work well together; C and D disliked each other so would not work well together; E and F would get on so well that they would be too busy chatting, so would get little work done. I took her good advice and the day went smoothly. Arthur Scargill and I had both been invited to speak at the school, which was held in a Durham hotel. I arranged and led the programme for the day, speaking at the start about the main arguments contained within the packs, while Arthur ended the day with one his brilliantly rousing speeches. I had been rather nervous about speaking in public in front of Arthur but felt reassured when he praised my talk afterwards. I also organised a national residential course (we called them schools) early in March 1984, so that more activist members would understand and make use of our *Campaign for Coal* materials.

What our coalfield publicity campaign needed was a complementary campaign aimed at newspapers and television channels. That was outside the remit of our staff campaign committee, but many of the points in our *Campaign for Coal* booklets could have helped us to win more public support. It would have been very helpful if mass media outlets had understood and explained how Government was depressing both the market for coal and its price when sold to the electricity industry.

There were two problems, though. Firstly, the NUM had only one press officer, Nell Myers, who was also Arthur's PA. Although Arthur was a skilled performer in the media, he had many other responsibilities too, while Coal Board and Government both had large PR teams. Secondly, media outlets rapidly became cheerleaders for the Government view of the mining industry and the NUM, so they were not often interested in our views of the industry.

Speaking at Moor Green in Nottinghamshire

Spring came both early and warm in 1984, so undermining the aim of our six-month-old overtime ban that was supposed to run down coal stocks. As the sun streamed into the windows at National Office, many of us were more sorry than glad because our cause was being damaged by the good weather. On one of those sunny days I took a call from Nev, a union branch official at Moor Green in Nottinghamshire, which had both a pit and a workshop.

"I'd like you to come and speak to the union branch. Could you come and talk about our campaign to save pits?"

"Yes, of course, I'd be glad to, but I need to know what's happening at Moor Green so I can work out how to approach it."

I knew how tense and divided the Notts coalfield was, thanks to media bias and some of the officials like Roy Lynk. He was campaigning vigorously and using personal attacks on National Officials to prevent the strike from really taking hold there.

"Well, it's difficult" said Nev. "We've got some of the lads on strike, and some of the lads working. So could you talk about the union's campaign without mentioning the strike?"

"All right, Nev, of course I'll come and speak. It won't be easy to avoid mentioning the strike, but I can talk about all the points in our *Campaign for Coal* packs. When do you want me to come?"

I was discovering that I quite enjoyed being asked to speak, but this meeting was going to be an exception. Walking on eggshells didn't begin to describe the job this time. I prepared a much more detailed script than usual for my talk, hoping that less improvisation would make it easier not to slip up and mention the strike. Trying, then, to stick close to the script, based on our *Campaign for Coal* booklets, I took the meeting through the economic need for coal; for new technology that would benefit miners; for carbon capture and storage instead of air pollution; combined heat and power to avoid heat wastage, then the rest of our campaigning points. Neither "strike" nor "industrial action" were words that crossed my lips that evening, despite what was going on around us. When you are speaking it is usually possible to read the audience, gauging their reaction, then adjusting content or delivery to meet their response.

Possibly as a sign of my unease, I just could not work out how my speech was going down. I guessed that at least some of the audience would still be working, despite the strike. There was polite applause at the end, then questions that I could answer – but what were they really thinking?

It remained a mystery to me, so when Nev rang me the following day:

"I'm not sure how it went down with the audience – what did you think?"

"Well, you convinced at least one of them – one of our younger members. He went home and told his dad, who works here too, that they should both be on strike."

"That's good, Nev, I'm glad."

"You've not heard the end of the story yet. His dad told him if he mentioned going on strike again, he'd throw him out of the house for good".

A pause.

"So the lad's still working."

Although I had intended to run a series of national residential schools, Leicester Area General Secretary Jack Jones scuppered my plans in spring 1984 by making an impassioned speech at the NEC, complaining that National Office staff were being used to further the strikes. Perhaps he was referring to the national school I had run in March, just as several strikes were breaking out, where we looked at our *Campaign for Coal* packs and our case for defending the coal industry. After that both Peter and Arthur insisted that I must abandon national schools for the time being. My time was then spent entirely on campaigning work, including writing and producing materials, organising meetings and rallies such as the rally outside the Special Delegate Conference in April 1984, then the Miners March on Mansfield the following month. I was also responsible for liaising, and if necessary supporting, the many miners' support groups, including women's groups, that were springing up.

5 Decision-making meetings One

First, a tale for snap-time: my overnight bag In Derbyshire and Notts pits, snap time is the name for the meal break in the middle of a shift. It is then that tales are told to pass the time as miners rest and eat the food they have taken underground.

I arrived in a taxi at the County Hotel in London the night before the October 1983 Special Delegate Conference with a group of Derbyshire miners and my boxes of *Campaign for Coal* packs. The Derbyshire delegates had promised to carry the packs to the conference in their shared taxi the following morning, as a shortage of rooms at the County had forced me to book into another hotel nearby. Almost straight away I met an old neighbour and friend Les Hardwick who worked at Pye Hill, so we sat down to chat. I dimly heard Derbyshire Area Secretary Gordon Butler offering to store my overnight bag for me while I enjoyed catching up with Les. After that, as Gordon and I seemed to be the only ones who had not eaten before climbing onto the train, the two of us went down the street to a Chinese restaurant. It was only as we walked back into the County Hotel that I realised my embarrassing position, because Mick McGahey was in the centre of a jovial group enjoying a few drinks in the bar, which spanned the space between the entrance hall and the stairs. Gordon had apparently stored my overnight bag in his room, so he and I would have to walk past that group together and go upstairs to collect it. As that would be bound to plant all sorts of ideas in the minds of the gossips, my best hope was to be as upfront as possible. As loudly as I could, I said

"It was kind of you to offer to store my bag for me, Gordon, but I need to collect it now so I can go round the corner to my hotel."

I could feel lots of pairs of eyes on both of us as we headed upstairs together. Why hadn't I paid more attention earlier, then I wouldn't have got myself into this embarrassing situation?

When we reached Gordon's room he invited me inside to collect my bag. As I was guessing there were several people in the bar who would be counting every minute I spent upstairs with him, I needed to get back downstairs as quickly as possible.

"No, thank you, Gordon, I need to get back to my hotel."

Probably guessing the reason for my embarrassment, he seemed to be teasing me. Grinning, he said

"You're not frightened of me, are you, Hilary?"

"No, no, of course not, it's just that I need to get back...."

After what felt like an age, he stepped inside the room and handed the bag over to me. I got myself downstairs as quickly as possible, then made a point of saying loud goodbyes to the group in the bar, so no one could fail to notice that I hadn't really spent much time upstairs with Gordon.

Special Delegate Conference October 21, 1983 in London By the time of that Special Conference, when it was clear that Margaret Thatcher's government was making another assault on the mining industry, the elected NUM President was Arthur Scargill, while Mick McGahey had been in place as Vice-president for some time. As well as the pressing issue of pit closures, there was an outstanding pay claim, which the Coal Board was blocking. Now that the left had more power within the union, with a left-wing President and Vice-president, the national leadership acted to harness together the intentions of Special Delegate Conferences and the actions of the National Executive Committee (NEC). This was a marked change from the approach of Joe Gormley, the previous President, who had used the National Executive Committee to overturn the decisions of both Conference and a national ballot when abandoning a key union policy that had led to national unity on pay. Under its new leadership, the NEC decided to call a Special Delegate Conference in October 1984 to discuss the urgent matters of both pay and pit closures.

I had taken advance copies of our new *Campaign for Coal* pack of information booklets to the Conference to provide key Area activists with our arguments in defence of the coal industry and jobs. Conference agreed to impose an overtime ban to reduce coal stocks and so strengthen our position as the anticipated dispute developed.

The stalled wage claim was also part of the reason for our overtime ban. That ban caused great loss of earnings for our members who worked as electricians and fitters, because they normally worked overtime at weekends so that coal production could re-start promptly on Mondays. Because it created all sorts of bottlenecks in production, individual colliery managers reacted in a number of ways, sometimes sparking various levels of industrial action by our members. In the four to six months leading up to the strikes, then, the situation in many pits was volatile, with coal production reduced. After that initial Special Delegate Conference, all further decisions about industrial action were also taken by delegate conferences, not by the National Executive Committee, nor by national officials, despite many claims to the contrary.

Special Delegate Conference April 19, 1983, in Sheffield By the time of this conference, Peter Heathfield, newly-elected as general secretary, had taken up his new post, with all three National Officials now left-wingers. Calling themselves the troika, they intended to work together, rather than against each other. They considered Special Delegate Conferences, made up mainly of lay members, to be the most democratic form of decision-making within our union. The April Delegate Conference was convened at Sheffield City Hall by our National Executive, which had already approved the existing strikes in Yorkshire and Scotland over colliery closures in their Areas. The thousands of members from many coalfields who gathered outside conference to lobby delegates were loud in their support for the strike. As about eighty percent of our members were thought to be on strike already, calling off those strikes in order to hold a ballot about whether to begin a national strike would have been a backward step. Instead conference agreed the use of an NUM rule allowing it to approve the existing Area strikes and call on the rest of the membership to join in. Conference also changed the rule about ballots for strike action, so that if any ballot were to be held in future, only a simple majority for strike action would be needed.

6 Marches and rallies

Chesterfield Early on in the strike a short rally was organised in Chesterfield, my own town, by the Trades Council, led by its President Barry Johnson. During that period, because of the local heavy industry, the Trades Council was an influential presence. Local trade unionists and members of the labour movement joined the march with great enthusiasm to show their support for the miners. NUM North Derbyshire Area, along with other Area leaderships, had called on their members to strike. The meeting, organised at short notice as a staging-post for miners travelling south to the Nottingham rally, was held outside Chesterfield town hall, with our speakers standing on the natural platform at the head of its entrance steps. With brightly-embroidered NUM Area banners held up behind them, Yorkshire NUM leader Jack Taylor spoke, together with Gordon Butler, Derbyshire NUM General Secretary. Barry included in his speech a tribute to the stalwart minority of Nottinghamshire miners who were striking. Someone, probably a Yorkshire miner, yelled: "Scabs!"

Never one to let a heckler score a point, Barry silenced him by saying: "It takes more courage to strike in Notts than in Areas where the strike is fully supported. Those Notts miners on strike are heroes, not scabs."

I could see Gordon Butler nodding in agreement. Local NUM officials, struggling themselves to win support for the strike in North Derbyshire, understood Barry's point only too well.

Nottingham The Nottingham march later that day was intended to encourage more Nottinghamshire miners to join the strike. Miners from many coalfields, with lots of supporters, gathered on Forest recreation ground so we could march into the city centre. As we travelled briskly downhill on the Mansfield Road, I was a long way back in the crowd, so I could hear the strikers' chant

"Here We Go, Here We Go, Here We Go…" drifting back up the hill. It felt good to be part of this large, lively crowd. There were also home-made placards and many printed posters, proclaiming Victory to the Miners, mounted on sticks. These were produced in large quantities during the strike by the Socialist Workers' Party, who were always good at raising their own profile while supporting other causes.

At that time striking miners and the NUM leadership were the darlings of almost the whole of the left in the labour movement. For instance Alan Meale, secretary of the Campaign Group of Labour MPs, promised me that their group would supply a speaker for NUM events in any place, at any time. That promise was never broken. I knew that my own MP Tony Benn and Dennis Skinner, MP for neighbouring Bolsover, toured the country to the point of near-exhaustion, trying to win support for the battle against pit closures. Labour Party leader Neil Kinnock, though, refused throughout the strike to speak on any of our platforms. Tony Benn's Diaries show the anger this caused among left-wing Labour MPs. Another exception to general support from the left for the miners, as the strike went on, were elements in the national leadership of the Communist Party, who became openly critical of the tactics of the NUM leadership. The Communist Party has always been under intensive surveillance and thus the government would have been aware of the sharp differences in the leadership and the sharp contradiction between the membership of the party, which was deeply involved in solidarity work with the miners, and the NUM's critics in the party leadership.

As we marched through Nottingham on that warm spring morning, though, I was unaware of all those machinations. Plenty of onlookers were enjoying this Saturday spectacle, yet I felt a sudden unease in my stomach: where were the stewards? Having only been involved in the organisation of the rally for a few days, I had assumed that stewards had already been organised by Roger Windsor, who seemed to be in charge of arrangements. Unable to see a steward anywhere, I needed to tackle the problem straight way. Looking around, I spotted Ian Juniper, a Nottingham trades council member and tireless activist in left-wing causes.

Finally reaching Ian, I had to speak over the noise of the crowd.

"We need stewards – can you help?"

The fleeting look of surprise on his face echoed my feelings.

"Yes, I know, I'll tell you more about that later."

It would never have crossed Ian's mind to refuse.

"Of course I'll help – what do you need?"

"We just need some experienced people to make sure we stick to our route and everything stays organised. Do you know anyone else who could help, as well?"

He identified a few other people from the Trades Council, so between us we managed to pull together some sort of team that would hopefully get us through the day. We were well past the point at which I could have collected them together for even a quick briefing, though.

As we neared the bottom of Mansfield Road, the cheerful atmosphere was suddenly wrecked. One of the leaders of the Kent NUM accosted Henry Richardson, leader of the Notts NUM, saying very loudly

'What's a scab like you doing here – you don't belong with us!'

Now it was true that the strike was being poorly supported overall in Notts. Henry, despite good intentions, was proving unable to lead most of his members into maintaining the strike because some other area officials, especially Roy Lynk, were actively working to sabotage it. Yet Henry was out on the march, showing his support for the strike on the streets of Nottingham, only to be insulted by a leader from one of the smallest coalfields in Britain. Several other marchers argued in defence of Henry against this verbal assault, but the super-militant from Kent seemed unaware of any point of view except his own. As a staff member it was not my place to comment openly, but privately I remembered how the labelling of Notts miners as "scabs" had been dealt with in Chesterfield that morning.

While we were still moving down Mansfield Road something happened to cheer me up after that unpleasantness. Frank Watters, a tireless back-stage worker for Arthur Scargill and the NUM, approached me, suggesting

"Why don't we organise a rally with speakers outside the Special Delegate Conference at Sheffield City Hall on Thursday? It will keep the lads occupied and out of trouble while they're waiting for the Conference decision to be announced."

"That's a really good idea, Frank – I'll talk to Arthur today and see what he thinks".

Meanwhile, there was still work to do in Nottingham. Once we arrived at the Albert Hall for our rally, a lot of miners crowded onto the speaking area in the middle of the hall. Some were drinking cans of beer to quench the thirst they had built up by walking in the heat. As it had already become clear that the press, TV and radio were hostile to the strike, I was worried. Visions of media images showing miners waving beer cans, accompanied by knocking copy about a drunken rabble of miners invading the city, wouldn't leave my mind. As soon as I could find Ian Juniper, I tried to sell him the idea that we needed to do something about it.

"We need to explain quietly to each man with a beer in his hand that the press and TV might misuse those shots they could take. Can you help by asking them quietly to put their drinks down or at least keep them out of sight?"

Ian said doubtfully

"They won't listen to me."

"Well, they'll listen to me" I said sharply, because I knew that somehow I had to persuade them to listen. So I quietly approached the nearest man with a can.

"Would you mind putting down your beer, or at least keeping it out of sight? If the media get hold of shots of miners waving drinks around, we'll be giving them an easy chance to have a go at us. We know they're against us."

"All right, luv, I see what you mean" as he looked around, spotting the press cameras.

I approached the next thirsty man in the same way, moving discreetly through the crowd while the meeting got under way. It seemed to work, as no adverse comments or images appeared in the media that weekend.

Sheffield 19 April 1984 The Special Delegate Conference in Sheffield, arranged to discuss strike action against proposed pit closures, would be a magnet for miners from almost every coalfield. It was an NUM tradition for members to gather outside important decision-making meetings to make their views clear to delegates; so even without a rally, thousands of our members would be demonstrating as delegates entered City Hall, then hanging about all morning waiting for the conference decision. Frank's idea would be a good way of getting the crowd through that long waiting period.

Although Arthur was keen on Frank's plan, I was the person who would have to turn the idea into reality. As nothing could be done until Monday morning when the working week for local authorities began, I had to work hard and fast to organise everything, from securing a rally space to organising a platform and speakers. For me, lunch breaks disappeared that week, while Judy, my faithful secretary, was also working at top speed.

First of all I needed the backing of council leader David Blunkett, a prominent figure in the "Socialist Republic of South Yorkshire". Keen to help, as he was at that time a committed socialist, he agreed to my request to close the designated car park outside City Hall to clear space for our rally. With David's support, it was easy to get council officers moving to create the necessary closure order for Thursday morning – the fastest action I ever saw by a local authority.

The next job was to find a firm that would erect a stage for us within our short timeframe. Yellow Pages led me to a company who said they could do the job very early on Thursday morning. To my surprise the young woman from Highway Scaffolding suggested a way of reducing the price.

"If we keep the platform below a certain height there's no need legally to put a safety rail around the edge" she said in a perky business voice, clearly expecting my gratitude for this money-saving tip. She seemed surprised when I bit back.

"There are going to be a lot of people at the rally and on that platform – our members and our full-time officials. I'll be up there myself. We take our members' safety very seriously, and anyway we need a high platform, but we'd want a safety rail even for a low platform."

"All right, if that's what you require," she said in an injured tone. She had not seemed to expect us to be concerned about safety. Ann Suddick had volunteered to help me set things up on Thursday morning. Secretary to the Durham Mechanics' area leader, Ann was a formidable organiser, devoted to the union, so I really appreciated her offer. She must have driven halfway through the night to reach Sheffield to join me at 6 o'clock that Thursday morning. We needed to ensure everything was in place before the large groups of miners began to arrive. As the conference starting time approached, so many had gathered on the car park that there were overspills onto surrounding streets. Their vivid silk union banners, painted and embroidered, too heavy to be held up all morning, were propped unfurled against walls. Some of our members even climbed onto a flat roof outside City Hall to get a better view of the platform. It was clear that these thousands of our members wanted the Special Delegate Conference to support strike action.

Throughout and beyond the following year, press and television outlets would imply time and again that many of our members had been dragged unwillingly into strike action. They claimed that "Arthur Scargill called the strike". This claim became so pervasive that at the time of writing, even the Working Class Museum Library website states "… on 12 March Arthur Scargill, president of the NUM, called a national strike". In truth, the National President had no power to call a strike, although like any other full time official he was free to make any rallying call to his members that he chose. What had really happened was that on 8 March, the National Executive Committee had agreed to the formal requests of Yorkshire and Scottish Areas that their existing strikes should be made official under NUM Rule 41. The Committee decided that any similar action in other Areas would also be made official. By the time of the April NEC meeting, more than 80% of our members were on strike through such Area decisions. That NEC meeting agreed to re-convene a Special Delegate Conference the following week, on April 19, to determine the next steps.

As a number of officials not due to attend the Special Conference had promised to speak outside at the rally, I hoped we would be able to keep things going until the conference ended. How difficult that turned out to be, as conference seemed to go on forever. Yet despite the hard work that had gone into organising it during the past four days, the rally could never be more than a sideshow. What all of us were desperate to hear was whether Conference would vote to support strike action against the planned pit closures. Ever since Thatcher's appointment of Ian MacGregor as NCB chairman, we had known that Thatcher's government was determined to seriously damage the coal industry. We knew of MacGregor's notorious union-busting activities in the US, where such attacks on union organisation often meant management's use of serious violence, including guns. We had seen his involvement in British Leyland, when union convenor Derek Robinson had been unfairly dismissed, then we had witnessed MacGregor's butchery of the British steel industry, with the loss of thousands of jobs. Our leaders and most of our members already understood that this was a battle for the very survival of the industry, our members' jobs and our mining communities.

For me, pressure to keep the rally going would be a good way of taking my mind off the agonising question of what Conference would decide. The miners who had come to lobby Conference were less lucky, though. Without an urgent job to distract them, all they had to think of was the Conference result. As the rally dragged on through the endless morning, private conversations, group jokes and all the usual bits of business developed within the crowd. They must have been very tired, as some of them had travelled half the night on buses from Scotland, South Wales, the North East or Kent.

During that morning I worked through every available NUM official, every trades council representative, every representative from other trade unions, every local councillor I could find to speak, yet still those damned City Hall doors stayed closed. During one speech, I was worrying about who I could find to speak next when Frank Watters helped me out of the hole. He brought a thick-set, light-haired man up onto the high platform.

"Hilary, this is Sean Cannon, one of the Dubliners. Sean, this is Hilary Cave, the union's education officer, who's organised this rally."

Was there anybody Frank didn't know? To be standing next to one of the Dubliners, shaking his hand, was an unexpected pleasure.

"Hello Sean, delighted to meet you. I'm a great fan of the Dubliners, and I've heard you perform here in Sheffield."

"Sean's willing to sing for us."

And was there anybody Frank couldn't get on our side?

"I could do a couple of songs for the crowd, if you like". He seemed a bit shy.

"That would be lovely – we'd be honoured, Sean."

As soon as the current speaker had done, I indicated to the chairman that I needed to borrow the microphone, then turned to Sean, my arm outstretched.

"And now, I'm delighted and honoured to be able to introduce Sean Cannon, one of the Dubliners. He's going to sing for us."

Judging by the applause and cheers, The Dubliners had plenty of fans in the crowd. I was the only one unable to enjoy his songs, though. While he was performing I was trying to identify another possible speaker to follow him, but I could see nobody who might do. Once Sean had stepped back from the microphone, with the crowd still applauding his songs, Frank spotted my metal NUM badge.

"What about giving Sean your NUM badge, as a thank-you", he suggested. Now Frank didn't know that my badge was a rejected prototype so I could never replace it. Although I didn't want to part with it, after such a generous gesture from a Dubliner, how could I even admit to such reluctance? So after just a moment of hesitation I unpinned it from the front of my coat and stuck it into Sean's lapel, thanking him again with what I hoped was my best smile.

As Sean and Frank left the platform I still had to keep the supply of speakers flowing. It was time to gamble. Pushing away the fear that this might turn out to be a mistake, I borrowed the microphone again, then asked

"Would anyone like to come up and speak?"

Following a bit of joshing, a smallish, fresh-complexioned man seemed to be pushed forward by his mates. He climbed the many steps onto our platform, which he described later as feeling like scaling Everest.

"Thanks for volunteering. Can you tell us your name, and where you're from?"

"George Bell, branch official from Shireoaks."

His accent showed him to be from the North East, one of many miners who had been obliged to move south in order to hang on to a job.

"Right, let's give George a big hand – it's not easy coming up here."

As he began, George handled the microphone well, keeping it close to his mouth and projecting his voice confidently. I began to relax a bit. He asked

"How do you get the whole of the South Yorkshire Police Force into a van?"

Pause for effect.

"Answer, you send in Chief Constable Peter Wright and everyone crawls up his arse!"

The crowd enjoyed that one. Already Yorkshire miners were beginning to dislike Peter Wright's attitude to them. Just two months later miners from across Britain would experience his approach to policing as they fled in fear from truncheon-wielding mounted police at Orgreave.

George remembers singing two Alex Glasgow songs – "Standing at the Door, at the Same Old Bloody Door" and "I Shall Cry Again".

While George was singing I had asked Sammy Thompson, a Yorkshire area official who had stayed on stage since his previous speech, to speak for a second time, and to carry on for as long as it took for Conference to end. I warned him that there were no other speakers available, so I was depending on him to keep things going. So that's what he was doing, until he suddenly stopped in mid-sentence, handing the microphone straight back to the rally chairman. Someone with a bigger ego would have wanted to finish his sentence, but Sammy, hewn from a better seam, had spotted delegates coming out of City Hall into the crowd. He knew we had to get the national officials up onto the stage as fast as possible to announce the Conference decisions.

Once we had told the crowd that the delegate conference decisions were about to be announced, everyone moved aside to let Arthur and Peter through. By the time they had climbed the steps and Arthur had taken the microphone, a tense quiet had fallen. He told them conference had voted not to hold a national ballot about strike action. Instead, delegates had voted to support the strikes already happening in various coalfields, and to urge all NUM members to join in. Delegates had also voted to require only a simple majority of votes in any future individual ballot about strike action. This was exactly what the thousands who had travelled to Sheffield wanted: determined and unified NUM action to protect their jobs and communities. They were delighted. It was only after I had told the crowd where to find their parked buses; warned them not to let the police provoke them; thanked Ann for her help; overseen the dismantling of the stage and begun to walk back to the office that I realised how worn out I felt. That feeling would become too familiar over the next year.

A tale for snap-time: John's babies Somehow on marches I kept bumping into the same man from one of the Coal Board workshops. Early in the strike he proudly showed me his baby. As there was no mother with them it was clear that John was enjoying looking after the baby himself. Towards the end of the strike he appeared with another baby, this time a very young one. As I admired this second baby he said earnestly

"You can see I haven't been wasting my time in the strike."

Looking at his face I could see that he wasn't joking, so I dare not even allow myself a smile as I agreed he hadn't been wasting his time.

London Lobby of Parliament Solidarity was on public show in London when we organised a demonstration and mass lobby of Parliament early in the summer of 1984. As we marched down Fleet Street with our banners we passed the distinctive Daily Express building, all black glass and steel. Venomous attacks on the miners had been written and printed there, yet on that morning of June 7 there was a crowd of workers outside, holding up circular messages of support, waving and cheering us on. It seemed that they were members of electricians' union EETPU, working at the Express. Defying their leader's virulent opposition to our strike, they had walked off the job to show their support for us. Heartened, of course we waved back enthusiastically.

I was thinking how well everything seemed to be going when I noticed Dennis Skinner, the NUM-sponsored MP for Bolsover. A former miner, Dennis had been wearing himself out travelling up and down the country to speak for the NUM. On that morning, though, he was clearly annoyed. On spotting me he demanded to know why he was not being allowed to speak at our rally in Jubilee Gardens, before we moved on to the Commons. "Well, Dennis, the plan is for just our National Officials to speak, along with someone from the Metropolitan Police Committee who's trying to hold the Met to account about human rights. We don't have time for many speakers because we need to get to Parliament in time for the lobby and the meeting in the Grand Committee Room. We hope you and other MPs will speak there."

He fixed me with one of his expertly angry glares.

"So why has Roger Windsor told Tony Benn he can speak at the rally in Jubilee Gardens?"

I was taken aback.

"I'm sorry, I don't know anything about that, Dennis. Just let me have a word with Roger to find out what's happened. I'll be back in a couple of minutes."

What on earth had Roger been doing? Was it some game he was playing? I quickly caught up with him.

"Dennis is angry – he says you've asked Tony to speak but he's been told that there's no time for him to speak. Has there been some misunderstanding?"

Roger muttered something I didn't catch.

"We need to get this sorted out – as Tony's been asked to speak, we can't really back out from that now. I suggest we ask Dennis to speak as well – it's the best we can do in the circumstances."

Roger agreed, so I went back to Dennis. I couldn't tell him that I suspected Roger had been playing games, so all I could manage was: "I'm really sorry, Dennis, there's been a misunderstanding. Of course we'd like you to speak in Jubilee Gardens, but time's short, so we're asking all the speakers to be brief."

I could understand why Dennis still felt slighted, but there was nothing more I could do. Once we arrived in Jubilee Gardens, I could see that it was well constructed for a rally. The only way onto the outdoor stage was through a gateway built into a brick wall, so we would not be troubled by a surge of journalists trying to get onto the stage. I stationed two stewards there, stressing

"The only people we want on the stage are our speakers. Don't let anyone else through, OK?"

One of our speakers was Paul Boateng, a Black civil rights lawyer and councillor, chair of the GLC Police Committee, who had been doing a valiant job trying to hold the Met to account. As the meeting went on, I began to worry that Paul had not yet appeared. Where could he be? I went behind the stage to speak to the lads at the gateway.

"Have you turned anyone away who said he'd been asked to speak? We've lost Paul Boateng."

"Well somebody came here, but we turned him away because he said he was from the Police."

Why hadn't I explained exactly who Paul was? I told the stewards the mistake wasn't their fault. I would try to find Paul, and if he came to the gate it was important to let him through straight away.

Back onstage, I managed to slip in an announcement, asking Paul Boateng to please come up to the stage. Hopefully, he wouldn't be too offended – I could do without having to smooth down a second person in one day who had been slighted. I was relieved when Paul appeared at the front of the crowd. So I could talk easily to him despite the current speaker's voice booming through the loudspeaker, I dropped into a sitting position, dangling my legs off the stage. As I began to apologise profusely for the mistake, he seemed to understand perfectly.

"Don't worry, these things happen."

"Would you like to speak now, Paul, just before we move on to Parliament?"

Seeming to sense my discomfort, he looked at me kindly, then

"Well thanks very much for the offer, but you've had a number of speakers, and you've got a strict timetable today. I think it's best if you leave me out now."

I shook his hand and thanked him once again, feeling grateful that he was putting our needs before his opportunity to shine in front of the large, friendly crowd. Once we had ended our rally and began to lead the crowd towards the House of Commons, it seems the police moved in and created some trouble. When some of our members were arrested, Paul Boateng showed his generosity by visiting them in the police cells so he could act for them.

The five rallies in November 1984 Late in 1984, when government and media attacks on the striking miners and the NUM had reached fever pitch, some miners were giving up and returning to work. Hunger and hardship, especially when it affected their children, were becoming harder to bear. The struggle to get the majority of Notts miners out on strike had been lost earlier on in the year, but in the other coalfields it was crucial to regain enthusiasm and keep up the numbers of striking miners, especially as Christmas approached. Trying to entice our strikers back to work, the Coal Board was making tempting offers of extra money for anyone who returned to work before Christmas. As the strike was clearly faltering the NUM's Executive Committee decided late in 1984 that we needed a series of rallies covering all our coalfields, instructing me to make this happen very quickly. The aim was to have all three National Officials speaking at each rally.

Back in my office, I realised what a huge job this was. It was easy to identify Sheffield and its City Hall as one venue that would be reachable from the Yorkshire, Derbyshire and Notts coalfields. I thought Birmingham and Newcastle were the other cities that would be accessible to our Midlands and North East members, but I would need to take advice from Areas about the best venues there. South Wales and Scotland each needed a meeting, but I had no idea of what the best towns, let alone venues, might be. As I set about consulting Area offices and securing bookings for halls, lunch breaks became a rare event, with my hardworking secretary Judy often bringing a sandwich to my desk.

Aberavon That rally has become infamous, written up afterwards with lurid sentences by eminent journalists. Martin Adeney and John Lloyd wrote "A noose dangled down from a catwalk over the head of Norman Willis", while Beckett and Hencke wrote "A noose was lowered over Willis's head..."

Daily Mirror journalist Geoff Goodman wrote "Shouting and interruptions increased accompanied by the grisly spectacle of a hangman's noose lowered slowly from the roof of the hall to within inches of Willis's face. There was uproar."

Now let me explain what really happened. Taking advice from the NUM Area, I had chosen the Aberavon Lido near Port Talbot as the South Wales venue. Because we would all be making lengthy journeys, I had ordered a very modest sandwich-and pork-pie buffet for our speakers and their staff before the start of the meeting. Of course anything lavish would have been wrong, in view of the hardships being endured by miners and their families, but we needed something to eat just to keep us going. Willis was the first speaker to arrive and although we had never met, I knew his reputation as a friendly and outgoing person. Yet when I shook his hand and thanked him for coming, I felt straight away that something was very wrong. Willis would hardly utter a word, despite my attempts at a friendly welcome. He ate almost nothing, but even if he and his driver had already eaten on their journey, that would not explain his manner. I found his coldness and unwillingness to talk both strange and uncomfortable. Only many years later did I discover that his wife was Neil Kinnock's PA. Throughout the strike Kinnock refused to speak on any of our NUM platforms, while years later he made at least one public statement about his contempt for Scargill.

Meanwhile, as with all the other November rallies, huge crowds were arriving. With the help of some branch officials I found a number of stewards for the meeting. Going into the sports centre manager's office to raise a question, I found him agitated, on the phone to the police, pleading with them to do something about the large crowds streaming into his centre for our meeting. He did not seem to be getting what he wanted. When the call ended he told me the police response was

"You're on your own, mate, but if you're worried about the numbers, just lock the doors".

So he did just that. Even with many people locked outside the building, the gym was very full, but Geoff Goodman's later claim of three thousand people present surely could not have been true. What gym in a local sports centre is big enough to hold three thousand people? Opening the rally, NUM South Wales President Emlyn Williams, who was chairing, welcomed Norman Willis in the usual brotherly manner. I was seated next to Jim, Arthur's driver, in an inconspicuous place on the temporary platform in the middle of the hall. As Willis began to speak his driver showed both of us a transcript of the speech so we could read it as Willis delivered it. That was how I knew every word the TUC General Secretary spoke had been prepared beforehand, presumably with Kinnock's approval or even involvement. Willis began with some brotherly comments, then moved on to criticise police violence on picket lines. Next he started to criticise our South Wales members in the hall for their alleged violence:

"I have marched proudly before many miners' banners – and I know that there will never be one that praises the brick, the bolt or the petrol bomb."

Yet there had been no bricks, bolts or petrol bombs anywhere in South Wales, which had been the most solid, and therefore the quietest, Area throughout the strike so far. What on earth was Willis doing, accusing our members in South Wales of violence? Looking around the hall I could sense that others felt the same: there was a restive atmosphere developing, although the meeting was still orderly. Then I noticed a stirring at the very edge of the sports hall, where a few climbing ropes were fixed to the ceiling. A young man, presumably a miner, seemed to be expressing without words his view of Willis's comments. He grabbed one of the ropes hanging down in front of him and shaped it into a circle, although he made no attempt at a knot, as you would expect on a hangman's noose. As he lifted his arms to raise the rope circle above his own head there was a general laugh, relieving some of the tension, with Willis himself laughing briefly, then continuing his speech. For that reason I could never believe Willis had felt truly threatened. The rope circle was never anywhere near Willis, as the rope was fixed to the ceiling at a far side of the hall, while the crowded platform was in the centre, surrounded by many people. There was no "catwalk" above our heads.

As the rally continued, with the usual brilliant speeches from our National Officials, Emlyn beckoned me over to the centre of the stage. He spoke very quietly so as not to disturb the speeches.

"We need to see that there are no unpleasant incidents with Norman – can you find some stewards to walk out of the hall with him at the end?"

I looked around, realising that most of stewards were scattered, unreachable, in the packed hall, so I stepped down into the crowd. Making my way with difficulty, I found a steward, a tall man I didn't know. Speaking softly, I said

"We need to form a little group around Normal Willis as he leaves the hall so would you join us, and can you find any others who'll help?"

He took my hand in his, looking me in the face. In one of those deep velvety Welsh voices he said

"I'd do anything for you, love – but not that!"

Trying again with others, somehow I assembled a little group of the willing, so at the end of the rally we surrounded Willis as he walked out of the sports hall. None of our members or supporters tried to accost or harm him, – indeed, they did not want to speak to him at all – but of course the media persons were in full ecstatic cry because the TUC General Secretary had accused the miners of violence.

Journalists and broadcasters were practically falling over themselves, and us, trying to approach him to ask for further quotes. I noticed that not one of them sought the views of Emlyn Williams, Scargill, Heathfield, or any of the miners.

Later my colleague Dave Feickert told me that as he watched the BBC TV news that night at home, he was puzzled by seeing Peter Heathfield on stage, apparently starting the rally with his jacket off, and ending the rally with his jacket on. Of course Peter had taken off his jacket as the meeting progressed, because the crowded sports hall was growing hotter and hotter. It seems that the BBC reversed their footage of the meeting, so giving a false impression of the atmosphere.

Were Adeney, Lloyd, Beckett, Hencke and Goodman actually there on the night? My guess is that they were not present. If they had been present, perhaps they should have launched into new careers as writers of fiction rather than journalism. But more than false words were created about that rally: I have even seen an online image, obviously faked, of a noose dangling over Willis's head, the noose showing a variety of moving loose ends prancing at odd angles from it. Such a creation would have been impossible to fashion from a sports centre rope fixed to the ceiling a long way from the stage. Those untrue accounts of that rally, universally believed, have taken on a life of their own. What I learned from the false stories written about that evening was to be sceptical about everything I see in print, even if written by eminent journalists such as the ones quoted above. In fact, Geoff Goodman of the *Daily Mirror* seemed to be pursuing his own agenda during the strike. I have seen a copy of a memo written to Margaret Thatcher by her press secretary Bernard Ingham, following a secret meeting between himself and trade union leader David Basnett during the strike. As Ingham's memo states that Geoff Goodman had set up the meeting, Goodman seems to have been operating well outside the normal duties of a journalist. Posing as a reporter of facts, he never admitted to his readers that he had arranged a secret meeting between the Prime Minister's aide and a trade union leader at that polarised time of national crisis.

Back in Aberavon, rooms had been booked in a local hotel, so during the evening I had rung them to ask if they could keep kitchen staff on duty to give us something to eat after the rally. They readily agreed, presumably pleased to have some well-known guests, but after the rally Arthur suddenly decided that we should go back home in case journalists declared us to be eating luxuriously while miners were going hungry. That meant I was forced to ring the hotel again, inventing a story that something urgent had cropped up which was forcing us to go back home. Apologising to the receptionist for our sudden no-show, I felt very uncomfortable. Arthur had simply changed his mind, so low-paid staff had been kept at work for hours, possibly without pay. We had another very long journey home that night. It was almost three in the morning before Jim dropped me off at home in Chesterfield, then he would have to drive for another forty-five minutes to leave Arthur at his door.

Birmingham After a very short night we were all back in Birmingham for the next rally. Nicholas Jones of BBC Radio Four interviewed Arthur, but as Arthur was also about to give a television interview, he and Jim were not yet free to travel to the rally venue. Because I needed to go there to oversee arrangements, Nick Jones kindly offered me a lift across the city. As National Office staff were not allowed to speak to journalists, I felt very uncomfortable, hardly daring to say a word in response to Nick's attempts at friendly chat. Although I felt guilty for my surliness, I dare not risk adverse headlines, or indeed my job, by saying something that I feared might be picked up and reported in a distorted way. In fact, Nick Jones was one of the better broadcasters, although I was unaware of that because, like most of the population, I did not listen to Radio Four news in those days.

Long before the time of the meeting there were crowds queuing outside Digbeth Civic Hall – it felt as though every member of the West Midlands labour movement was keen to hear our national officials speak. Standing outside the door for a few minutes, viewing the crowd, I heard that several bus-loads of our members were still on their way. I began to worry there might not be room for them once all these other keen supporters had gone inside. So I spoke to the crowd, asking them to stand back for a while to ensure all our members and their families could find seats first. People queuing passed that message back to others, so the crowd co-operated in a good-natured way and in the end there was room for everyone.

Lots of media persons had turned up, clearly hoping for a re-run of the previous night's attack on our members. Standing on stage as the rally began, I could see camera operators spread out on the floors of the aisles in the hall, trying for a novel camera angle. That night the TUC speaker was Bill Keys, a member of the TUC General Council and leader of one of the print unions that had been offering us marvellous solidarity all the way through the strike. When Bill spoke he gave us the complete support for our struggle that we felt we deserved, which delighted the crowd, so I looked forward to seeing the following day's headlines and news bulletins. To my surprise and disgust Bill's support was not mentioned by mainstream media. I learned then that if you say what the newspaper owners, TV managers and Government want to hear, your comments will be trumpeted loudly. Say what they do not want to hear and you will be ignored, in effect silenced.

Edinburgh Following advice from the capable Ella, Mick McGahey's PA, I had booked the Usher Hall in Edinburgh for our rally in Scotland. As miners and their families poured in through the entrance I was accosted by a woman who seemed to work in the ticket office. It was clear from her words, tone and expression that she did not think these people were the type who deserved to enter the hallowed portals of the Usher Hall. She wanted me to ask "Mr McGahey" if he was happy for "these people" to come inside.

This revealed how highly respected Mick McGahey was, even in a place like the Usher Hall. It also indicated the prejudice against working class people that existed in this haunt of the cultured middle classes. Realising that I would be unable to shift her entrenched views within the next couple of minutes, I hid my anger at her appalling attitude towards our members and their families.

Reluctantly, I promised to consult "Mr McGahey" about her query. Of course I had no intention of doing so. How could I ask him if our members, who paid his salary and mine, were fit persons to enter the Usher Hall? Seething inwardly, I left her sight for a few minutes. Back in the foyer again, I pretended to have consulted Mick, assuring her he was happy for our members to come in. She kept quiet after that. As usual, the rally was very successful and well-attended. We stayed in a hotel, used regularly by the NUM, that seemed to be a long drive away from the venue. As Jim drove me to the station next morning we listened to BBC Radio Scotland. I was impressed by their fair and accurate reporting of our rally, which was very different from what I was hearing from the BBC at home. I began to realise then that Scotland really was another country.

Sheffield On the afternoon of the Sheffield rally I walked over to City Hall so I could liaise with Special Branch, who had insisted on bringing in sniffer dogs to check that no bombs had been planted. While I enjoyed the irony of this sudden concern for our welfare, I was not relishing the prospect of polite discussions with senior police officers.

As I watched the sniffer dogs, led by handlers, working their way along rows of seats, a senior Special Branch man approached and, once he understood that I was the event organiser, offered a handshake that I returned without enthusiasm. Apparently eager to talk – perhaps hoping for something to put on file – he opened with

"What's that badge on your lapel? I haven't seen one of those before."

"It's nothing much."

"No, tell me, I'd really like to know."

"You won't like it."

"I'm really interested – it's so unusual."

This was becoming tedious. Here we go, then...

"It's an Orgreave veteran's badge, given only to those who were there on that day."

His sharp response was immediate:

"I was on leave that day!"

It's strange, I thought, not one of them ever admits to having been there on that day. So who were those stave-wielding, galloping horsemen from whom we had fled in such fear?

As I expected the Sheffield rally to be well-attended because of its location, I had booked the main City Hall and an overflow hall below it, so those in the overflow space could watch proceedings via closed-circuit TV. Even with that overflow hall full, there were lots of people outside for whom we had no space. Phil Thompson, one of the Yorkshire Area office staff, approached me before the rally began, asking if there was anything he could do to help. As we already had stewards on stage and in both halls, I asked him to go into a little crow's nest space well above the stage, so he could see out into the audience and spot any potential problems. With the bright stage lights on, it was hard for those of us lower down onstage to see into the auditorium. Phil did this job happily and I was touched by his desire to help. Once more, journalists were keen to come onstage in hope of finding a story. One was a reporter from North Derbyshire who had previously made his name with a scoop unconnected with our industry. That night Jean McCrindle, a prominent person in Women Against Pit Closures, was onstage, probably because she was due to speak at the rally. As soon as she spotted this reporter she became very agitated.

"What's he doing here – he wrote a story about me and I've been getting death threats ever since…"

Jean was clearly upset, so I asked the reporter to leave the stage. As he didn't do so straight away I called over some stewards. Once they began to approach he started walking backwards, then tripped and fell, but luckily only his dignity was hurt, so he picked himself up and left reluctantly. That rally was another great success.

Newcastle Almost as soon as I arrived at the Newcastle rally venue, I realised that my choice of Sunday evening for our rally there had been a mistake. One of our members told me, with a grin to show he was teasing, that Sunday was a religious day. Another was more direct: he pointed out that, as Sunday evening was when they took their wives out for drinks, it was not their favourite night for a rally. But by then it was too late to change the day. Everything was set up and ready, except that Arthur had not yet arrived. I knew he was making a very long car journey but in 1984, before everyone had mobile phones, it was not possible for us to know exactly where he was.

In the end we started the meeting late, with Arthur still absent. I kept conferring with leaders of the local Area about what we should do and finally, in desperation, we decided that once the current speaker had finished, we ought to announce that Arthur was not able to attend after all. Then I was approached by one of the many police officers who had been hanging about all evening. He said

"Mr Scargill's at such and such a place, so he'll be here in twenty minutes".

When I asked how they could possibly know that, he told me they had used what were then called walky-talkies to track Arthur as he was driven up North. Although I found that heavy monitoring chilling, it was useful to know that Arthur would arrive in time to speak after all. As the police prediction was accurate, he was just able to slide into the slot reserved for the last speaker. That was the only time during the entire strike when I saw the police offer us any assistance.

All our five rallies had been extremely successful in attracting capacity crowds, boosting the morale of our members, officials and staff, as well as encouraging our labour movement supporters. I cannot recall any evidence, though, that they boosted the numbers of strikers, which was the reason I had been instructed to organise them.

London February 24, 1985 Long before then our National Executive Committee had been focused solely on trying to settle the dispute, but as the Government did not want to settle, we were making no progress. Many years later Seamas Milne uncovered a memo sent early in the strike by the Prime Minister's semi-secret asset David Hart to MacGregor and Thatcher, stating that the NUM strikers must be forced back to work without a settlement. It was not surprising, then, that Thatcher and her cohorts did not want meaningful negotiations.

In late February 1985 the Liaison Committee for the Defence of Trades Unions, and the South East Region of the TUC, organised a huge march in London to support us. Many people had brought their children along. My partner Barry Johnson and I had travelled to London in a bus chartered by the NUM Arkwright branch. I can remember that we had been halted as we marched along Whitehall. Something was wrong, though: suddenly there were lots of mounted police, who seemed to be forming up for a cavalry charge. Surely, surely, even the Met wouldn't mount a cavalry charge against a crowd containing lots of children? But that was exactly what seemed to be about to happen.

Barry positioned himself in front of me, his feet wide apart, to try to protect me. I found that touching, although my experience at Orgreave had taught me that when the police mount a cavalry charge there's only one thing to do: run. In the tense hush a samba band from Sheffield started playing the Internationale, which cheered us all up. When I try to recall what happened next, my mind is blank. I can remember very clearly what happened at Orgreave, but somehow I cannot remember what happened in Whitehall, except that I feel weepy when I try to think about it. The next thing I remember is that we were all sitting in our bus, which was parked just off Whitehall, with some trouble around us on the street. We were safe, though, as even the Met wouldn't fancy their chances mounting a cavalry charge against a bus. We could see a pile of crash barriers stored nearby, then some people started running up and carting them away, presumably for protection against the police horses. Police arrived and began to arrest those people.

As they were starting to shove one man into a police van an inspector appeared, pushed two leather-gloved fingers very quickly into the man's eyes then withdrew them instantly. It looked like a well-practised assault. Although it must have been very painful for the arrested man, that fast attack would normally have been invisible to anyone else. Because of our position high in the bus seats, we could see exactly what was happening. We were all commenting angrily on what we had seen, but not one of us was surprised because back in our coalfield we had all become used to the appalling way the Met behaved.

Thinking about that day, and puzzled by the gap in my memory, I began to ask around, hoping to find someone else who had been there. Jill Brunt of Chesterfield then uncovered online information that showed there had been a lot of trouble, including police cavalry charges. That led me to Tony Benn's *Diaries*, where he stated that 100,000 had been present at Hyde Park for the initial rally. Tony noted that, once some of the marchers had reached Trafalgar Square, the police had moved in and stopped the end of the procession from getting near to the Square. That would explain my memory of standing about in Whitehall, as we would have been in that part of the crowd which was prevented from reaching Trafalgar Square.

Tony wrote that police had launched both baton attacks and charges by mounted officers. So the answer to my previous question was yes: the Met did charge on horses against a crowd with many children in it. Even thinking about it now I feel emotional. If I had been so traumatised that my memory blocked out what had happened when I saw children attacked in that way, what must those children have suffered? Trying to describe police actions that day, the only word I can find is "wicked".

7 State power weaponised against us

Social Security Once our strike began, single strikers found they were entitled to zero social security pay. The regulations falsely assumed that strikers would receive £15, later £16, weekly from their union in strike pay. Government was aware that this assumption was false, yet it fitted the Ridley Plan ethos of washing the state's hands of responsibility for paying strikers. The NUM had no history of giving strike pay to our huge membership, so in real life, families had to live on state benefits set at pittance level under the pretence that their usual breadwinner had ceased to exist. As these supposed ghosts still needed food and clothing, families had to stretch a paltry amount of money even further.

Forty years later the wife of a former miner still remembers bitterly that to provide for her family, including herself and her husband, a four-year old child and a baby she received £11.75 each week. Another Derbyshire mining family still remembers receiving between £13 and £15 each week for a family with two children and a baby. I heard of at least two miners' families who were reduced to selling some of their basic household goods on Chesterfield flea market. Alterations to benefit regulations, which Government could implement without a vote in Parliament, ensured that death grants were not payable to strikers' families. That led to heartbreaking cases such as the family who had to bury their baby in someone else's coffin because they could not afford to buy their own. There was such an outcry about similar cases that the government adjusted its rules, although the new regulations did not in fact make life easier for strikers' families. David Willetts, an adviser in Thatcher's Policy Unit, pointed out to the politicians

"It would be politically neat to bring out one amendment which both gave concessions for funeral expenses and tightened up the regime for mortgage interest payments."

So Willetts persuaded the Government to relax one cruel social security rule while another was being tightened, making it much harder to access money to keep up mortgage interest payments. In due course Willetts was rewarded for this underhand piece of meanness by his adoption as a Tory parliamentary candidate, his promotion to ministerial rank, then his elevation to the House of Lords, where he still sits. Generous pay for MPs, ministerial salaries and perks, followed by the largesse of the House of Lords payment system, have all guaranteed him a comfortable life for the past forty years. During the 1984-5 strike his advice to government about how to tighten the financial screws on mining families caused such terrible hardship that mining families sometimes broke apart under the strain. Miner's wife Kate Alvey has spoken publicly about the painful effects on family life of Willetts' "politically neat" proposal. She recalled that because she had a part-time job the family's state benefits amounted to a Giro for nineteen pence, although they had two young children. Their mortgage repayments grew so far in arrears that the company threatened to repossess their home, sending people round to measure it up as part of that process. Her husband remained on strike with her full support and her enduring involvement in the Chesterfield Women's Action Group, but not every family was able to maintain its resolve and survive under those enormous pressures.

Poverty was not the only enemy of family life. The vicious government abuse being hurled at our strikers, amplified with relish by mass media, sometimes encouraged or even caused women to leave their men who stayed out on strike. This was a particular problem in Nottinghamshire, our second largest coalfield, where the strike was always weak. There, such abandoned men were sent for support to the women's groups, whose approach to consolation I privately though could only be described as very bracing. They would tell the men: if she's left you because you're on strike then she's not worth anything anyway....

Monopolies and Mergers Commission (MMC) Report Our more innocent citizens might have believed the Monopolies and Mergers Commission to be protecting us from possible abuses by big business, but in fact it was used to attack the nationalised coal industry instead. Government instructed the MMC to investigate whether the Coal Board could improve its efficiency and so reduce costs. The Commission recommended both pit closures and reorganisation of the industry into smaller accounting units, which would make it easier to claim that a particular pit was uneconomic. Government refused to acknowledge that a particular colliery could appear uneconomic at one point, if geological problems had cropped up or expensive new equipment had just been installed, yet the same pit could switch quickly to showing a profit once production increased because of investment, or because a geological problem had been overcome. Although more investment tended to bring increased production and better financial returns, government had been under-investing in the coal industry for a long time. Their aim, to close many collieries and privatise the rest, was driven by an ideology that today we call neoliberalism. Crudely expressed, they believed that private business was always good, while nationalised industries were merely a damaging drain on the public purse.

Market and accounting manipulations All sorts of ploys were adopted by Government to hide a realistic view of our industry. The nationalised electricity industry was the biggest buyer of coal, so the price paid by the Central Electricity Generating Board (CEGB), had a huge impact upon the finances of the nationalised coal industry. In a time when the Government was increasingly focused solely on the financial performance of nationalised industries, political interventions in the market ensured that the price of coal was kept down while the price of electricity was maintained at a high level. From 1982 to 1983 the price of coal bought from the Coal Board by CEGB to fire its power stations rose by only 4.7%, while the price at which CEGB sold electricity to its customers rose by 8.1%. That meant the electricity industry appeared to be profitable while the coal industry appeared to be loss-making, merely through manipulation of market pricing. Government also undermined the position of the coal industry by quietly funding the huge expense of converting those same power stations to burn oil as well as coal, so weakening our bargaining power when our members stopped work. A Cabinet paper from the 1970's, only opened to the public many years later, shows that one of Government's cited reasons for favouring nuclear power over coal was that this would reduce the power of the mining unions. It was no surprise, then, to find that Thatcher's Policy Unit was packed with pro-nuclear staff. Government never admitted that British Coal production costs were the lowest within the European Economic Community, while our coal industry received less government subsidy per tonne than was allocated in any of those other countries. Jack Smith, Assistant Area Transport Manager for the Coal Board in North Derbyshire, was told that the European Economic Community had offered to provide the Coal Board with extra funding so British coal production could be subsidised more heavily. It seems that offer was never taken up. After all, as the British Government plan was to reduce then privatise the industry, why would they want to strengthen the finances of the industry while it was still nationalised? As Margaret Thatcher claimed publicly that there was no such thing as society, her Government's neoliberal ideology would never allow Ministers to consider the terrible economic and social costs of pit closures, costs which are still being borne today by former mining communities.

Following the plan set out in the Ridley Report, Government instructed the Coal Board to deliver extra quantities of coal to build up stocks at power stations, so Jack Smith felt sure then that Government was preparing for a strike. As a member of management union BACM he himself would not be called upon to strike. Jack was told by CEGB that Government had handed them £60 million to build up coal stocks at power stations. At a time when they claimed the coal industry was costing too much, Government was prepared to expend huge sums on defeating the NUM's attempts to save the industry and their jobs. Jack organised the extra coal deliveries to power stations, as requested. Because he could see his drivers facing a lean time in the near future he advised them to put their overtime earnings away safely, rather than spending them.

Once the strike began Coal Board lorry drivers in Derbyshire, all NUM members, were no longer working, while the rail unions were refusing to move coal. The only exceptions made by rail unions were for trainloads approved by NUM for use in hospitals or old people's care homes. As strike-breaking "working miners" in key Midlands Areas were still producing coal, private haulage companies were heading for a bonanza. As we shall see in the Wheels of Justice section below, that bonanza came at a potential cost to public safety. Jack Smith was aware of a haulage company whose owners made a huge sum of money from driving coal to South Wales steel and coking plants. The company's owner displayed on his office wall a framed letter of thanks and a photograph from Margaret Thatcher herself. Eventually they made so much money from driving scab coal that they retired to the Channel Islands on the advice of their accountants.

Once different units of the NCB began to be treated as separate financial entities, following recommendations of the Monopolies and Mergers Commission, it became easier to claim that individual collieries or units were uneconomic, and therefore should be closed. Jack Smith had always allocated transport charges to different units based on origins and destinations of the journeys. Suddenly he was told to charge a particular job to a totally unconnected unit. When he said that would not be appropriate, as the unit had not been involved in the transport operation, so should not be charged for it, he was told that he was being given a firm instruction, not a request. Jack realised the figures were being manipulated to make it appear that certain units were loss-making.

Policing centralised and politicised   A former manager in the Orgreave Coking Plant has pointed out that, well before the strike had begun, police had visited the site to discuss future policing plans with management. Most of us, unaware of such advance activities, only realised once the strike had begun that radical changes were being made in policing. Thatcher was always demanding that the police do more against the strikers. Near the start of the strike she was reported to have literally banged on the table at a meeting with police chiefs, telling them they must stiffen their resolve when dealing with the miners. In theory each individual police force is considered a separate entity, although a Chief Constable may request support from other forces. Chief Constables have always had complete control over operational decisions in their own areas. Both Police Committees (made up of local councillors and magistrates) and the Home Office are responsible for part-financing the bills for such decisions. In the early 1980's it seemed that the only Local Authority attempting to hold its police force to account was the Greater London Council (GLC), whose Police Committee Chairperson was lawyer Councillor Paul Boateng. Following the 1972 miners' strike a body called the National Reporting Centre (NRC) had been set up to enable Chief Constables to request officers from other forces to support their operations. Run by the Association of Chief Police Officers (ACPO), it became a powerful entity that, in terms of policing the strike, seemed to us to unify all police forces into a single anti-strike weapon. That view is supported by the notorious incident when police, using the NRC to track a busload of picketing Kent miners, stopped them entering the Dartford Tunnel, forcing them to return to base. NRC planned and co-ordinated police reinforcements travelling between various constabularies, with the huge size of that operation revealed by the fact that all 43 police forces in England and Wales became either givers or takers of reinforcements who crossed constabulary borders during the strike. Between 4000 and 8000 officers were said to have been deployed in a co-ordinated way every day by NRC.

Chief Constables had no power to refuse to supply such reinforcements to other Constabularies if asked to do so, but their Local Authorities would then request payment from the "receiving" Authority. Because of their budget problems, many Authorities tried to pressure the Home Office into footing a higher portion of those bills for outside help. Derbyshire took the uniquely firm line of refusing to pay any bill from an outside police force, on the grounds that their Police Committee had not been consulted about whether other forces should operate within their boundaries. At a meeting with the Chief Constable, held in public, Derbyshire County Council Leader David Bookbinder was forthright about their position. He stated that any other Local Authorities which sent police into Derbyshire should be aware that they would receive no payment for such exports. Years later friends of Bookbinder, affectionately known to many as Bookie, recalled that he was then summoned to Downing Street for a personal meeting with Thatcher. With her unique blend of vindictiveness and self-righteousness, she gave him a stern telling-off. Bookbinder invited her to tell him what statute he was breaking by refusing to pay outside police forces for coming into Derbyshire, when his own Police Committee had played no part in the decision to summon them. As she was unable to name any law he was breaking, he won his point. Presumably because the Government did not want a public fuss that would reveal how many thousands of police were involved in the strike, nor did they want to publicise the huge sums of money that were being spent, they stopped harassing him. The bills were never paid.

Police and coalfield communities Across the coalfields police vehicles suddenly sported numbers painted on their roofs, so helicopters could track their progress. Those numbers, allocated by the National Reporting Centre, were part of a national series of identification marks, illustrating the move to a national policing structure. While police vehicles were gaining identifying numbers, individual police officers were often mysteriously losing theirs. Regulations stated that officers must display numbers on their shoulders, but we often noticed the absence of such identifying marks, especially when officers were anywhere near collieries or pickets. Police behaviour was often so bad that in normal times there would have been many complaints against them, but it was impossible to complain about the behaviour of police officers if you could not cite their numbers. Our members realised very soon that there was no point in even trying to complain about individuals because the mindset of an occupying army became the driving force of the entire police operation.

NUM members, staff and officials were not the only people the police tried to prevent from conducting their lawful business in coalfield areas at that time. It became difficult or impossible to travel into Nottinghamshire, or even within Derbyshire near the Notts border, with police road blocks at M1 Junctions 28 and 29, supplemented by road blocks on more minor routes. John McCabe, who was not a miner, was a Nottingham Forest football fan living in Derbyshire's Amber Valley. Driving to the Forest ground very early one morning, he was hurrying to join a coach full of fans who would be travelling abroad to watch their team. Stopped at a police road block near the former Babbington pit on the outskirts of Nottingham, he was forced to produce his passport and ticket for the foreign football match before being allowed to continue his journey. All the time he was hoping desperately that the delay would not make him miss his coach.

Graham Skinner and Stuart Ashmore, both Clerks of Works for Derbyshire County Council Highways Department, had been in Eckington inspecting road construction works. They drove onto the M1 at Barlborough Junction 30, heading South. When they reached M1 Heath

Junction 29 they found a line of police stopping traffic. An officer asked where they had come from and where they were heading. Ian said they were going to the Surveyor's office in Clay Cross, but the policeman, accusing them of being flying pickets, forced them to drive North again to Barlborough, encouraging them on their way with the polite instruction "Fuck off back to Yorkshire!"

Graham recalled "Of course the same thing happened when we tried to get off at Barlborough, but were not allowed to, and back to Heath Junction we went again. I looked at the petrol gauge. The same line of coppers were there. "You again?" they said. We then told them to allow us into the County Council Highways Maintenance Depot at Heath, next to Junction 29. They would verify who we were. We added that we were running low on petrol, so if we were sent back to Barlborough we could break down on the M1. Then came another copper who was concerned about traffic buildup behind us and told us to "fuck off" but didn't say where. So we drove off from Heath Junction to the pretty charming (by then) Clay Cross."

Imagine that level of harassment for a whole year when you are simply trying to do your job.

Some miners believed that the absence of numbers on police uniforms indicated that they were soldiers rather than police. There were often reports, difficult to prove or disprove, from miners who said they had recognised soldiers they knew who were standing on police lines in police uniforms. In summer 1984, when we held a mass lobby of Parliament, I was inside the House of Commons, where a friendly MP had booked the Grand Committee Room so we could hold a meeting there. One of the MPs beckoned me to a window, where we could see police handling some of our people, including women, very roughly as they queued to see their MPs. We were very concerned, but as it was a lengthy walk from where we were to the outside queue, it was hard to know what we could do to help. In any case, the attempted intervention of an MP held no guarantee of success, as NUM-sponsored MP Kevin Barron had his arm broken by a police officer when he visited a picket line at Maltby.

What we could not see from the Grand Committee Room was another drama being played out in that crowd. One of our members, an amateur photographer, spotted a man wearing the uniform of an army sergeant sitting in the driver's seat of a parked police van. He took a picture but realised straight away that police officers had spotted what he was doing, and they were moving through the big crowd towards him. In those days before digital cameras were in general use all film came in rolls. Our member took his film out of the camera, rolled it into a canister then tossed it into the crowd, calling out "Get that to the NUM". When the police finally reached him through the crush they seized his camera but found they were too late, as the film had disappeared. Someone in the crowd must have responded to his shouted plea because the film found its way to Maurice Jones, editor of our newspaper *The Miner*. That photo of an army sergeant in the driver's seat of a police van appeared on the front page, with the caption "Gotcha!". That word was copied from one of the *Sun's* unpleasantly crowing headlines from the Falklands War, when our navy had sunk the Argentinian ship Belgrano with great loss of Argentinian life. To us that photograph was the smoking gun that proved army personnel were being infiltrated into the police, but the official response was bland. It was said there had been a bomb scare so the army, not wanting to alarm the public, had borrowed a police van to deal with the threat. Although we did not believe their story, our accusation was never taken up by mainstream media.

In another place entirely there was an incident suggesting the same sort of armed forces influx into police lines. Barry Johnson, President of Chesterfield Trades Council, joined the Linby picket line as usual near his home in South Notts very early one morning. A man in police uniform instructed the pickets aggressively to get back behind a wall. Barry said loudly "I bet that makes him feel a lot better".

The man in police uniform threatened to arrest him, so Barry asked
"What for?
The reply was
"For insulting the Queen's uniform."

That expression sounded odd coming from someone in a police uniform because it is an armed forces expression, rather than a term used by police. Paul Johnson of North Derbyshire recalls that his brother, a military policeman serving in Germany, was instructed to go back to Britain taking a number of white shirts with him. He was told that he would be working on picket lines as a police officer. Although Paul's brother refused such a duty because he had several relatives who were striking miners, he suffered no penalty for his refusal to carry out an order. That suggested his commanders did not want to make an issue out of their instruction.

On duty outside collieries to prevent any effective picketing, police officers often taunted our striking members, waving fivers in their faces. They would laugh as they bragged about how much overtime money they were making out of the strike. Many striking miners and coalfield women have memories of brutal police behaviour, with the Metropolitan Police always identified as giving out the worst punishment. There are lots of stories from Notts pit villages about Met officers. On at least one occasion during a police incursion into a village, a striking miner was captured, his arms pulled around a lamp post and his wrists handcuffed so he could not move. He was then abandoned in the street, with a sticker posted onto his clothing proclaiming "I've met the Met."

Derbyshire striking miner Paul Johnson was at a picket where Met police were assaulting them. As a qualified first aider he diagnosed a fellow picket, lying on the ground, as having a fractured femur, so he was trying to bind both the man's legs together to support the fractured limb until he could get more medical help. Met officers instructed him to stop that, so he protested that the man needed looking after because of his broken femur.

"We'll take care of him" they said. Paul recalled with disgust that the Met's way of taking care of the seriously injured man was to push him down the bank so as he travelled downwards, laid on the ground, he was crying out with the pain of his fractured femur. Betty Cook of South Yorkshire, a small, slight woman, had her knee fractured by a police truncheon, while one of the North Derbyshire Women's Action Group had a tooth knocked out by a police officer who hit her in the face.

Dennis Clayton was travelling in a minibus full of workmates, including women, one day to a meeting. Apparently their Coal Not Dole window stickers offended the police, so they were stopped at Pleasley near M1 Junction 28 and accused of being pickets. Refusing to turn back, they were placed into a police mobile cell block, or pod van. Those vehicles, used for carrying people between prisons and courts, always seemed to me to be a punishment in themselves. Each person was isolated in a tiny compartment called a pod, unable to see out of its small high barred window, with just a flat metal stool, fixed to the floor, to sit on. Because one of the women was found to be carrying over-the-counter painkillers in her bag, all the women's bags were searched. Perhaps the police thought her painkillers, carried by huge numbers of women, indicated that she was a dangerous drug addict or dealer. This prison vehicle was then driven to Mansfield, where they were kept for hours without food or drink. Many years later Dennis was forced to clear his name when he applied to be a volunteer driver for a County Council mental health project. He was told that there were "black marks on his record" that might make him unfit for that volunteering task so he asked when they occurred. When told they related to events during 1984-5 Dennis explained what had happened and was then cleared for the volunteer driving role he wanted.

Oppressive police behaviour became the norm in coalfield areas during the strike. Early one summer morning a group of pickets, men and women, travelled a short distance from Shireoaks to Harworth in the South Yorkshire Coal Board Area. One of their leaders was George Bell, a branch official. There was a large police presence, and as they approached the pit they were stopped by a constable who said they were not allowed to picket there. George's response was

"My father fought against fascism in the Second World War in order to give us cherished freedoms, including the right to protest."

George's eloquence failed to stir the conscience of the policeman.

"Before I knew what was happening this copper – he was so young he hadn't even got stubble on his cheek – 'ad me 'and up be'ind me back, telling me I was nicked. They put me and the others, including women, into a mobile cell block. We were there for hours and it got hotter and hotter. We had no food, no water and no toilet facilities. I could hear some of the women shouting and crying. It was late evening before they took us to Mansfield and put us in front of a magistrate, who bound us over. A solicitor came, but we weren't released until after midnight."

They were also a long way from their homes in the far north of the county. Despite the danger of more legal trouble that could lead to dismissal George, like many other NUM members, kept on picketing while waiting for his case to come to court three months later. This time he was summonsed to appear in Worksop, where magistrates then said they could not hear the case because they already knew George from his standing and positions within the community. There were further delays, perhaps because the police officer could not be spared from his duties, or because his Hampshire force did not want to pay his fares. After all, once the strike had been defeated the state no longer considered miners a threat. Six months after the strike had ended the case against George and his group was finally to be heard in court. Their solicitor pointed out that if they agreed to be bound over, they would be able to watch the police destroy their fingerprints, taken on the day of their arrest. The problem with being bound over was that you had to admit guilt. George said he wanted to clear his name completely as he had not been obstructing the police officer in the course of his duty. The other defendants, men and women, voted to be bound over, so George was obliged to go along with the majority decision. All he managed to do was to create a little stir as his fingerprints were being destroyed, by asking what was happening to the other set of his prints that he reckoned the police had hidden away.

Before the creation of the Crown Prosecution Service, the police themselves undertook prosecutions. During the strike it seemed to be standard practice for police to decide what bail conditions should be imposed before the magistrates had even heard the case, let alone reached their verdict. Magistrates would then tamely accept those pre-determined conditions, which according to Steve Brunt meant, in the Chesterfield area, miners were only allowed to picket their own pits. Miners from other areas recall bail conditions that forbade them from going near any Coal Board establishment including their own workplace. The authorities saw that as an easy way to reduce the number of pickets available.

What they had not anticipated was the extent to which women instead of men would join the picket lines, especially if their own partners were officially forbidden from picketing. So bans on picketing for those arrested often served only to widen the pool of available pickets, with local women's support groups undertaking picketing on top of their other vital work. The police could find women on picket lines harder to control than men, because often those women did not work at the collieries. As men employed by the Coal Board knew they might be sacked if they got into even minor trouble with the police, the women felt they had more freedom to resist the police. Those officers, often rude and bullying towards striking miners, seemed to reserve their deepest contempt for coalfield women. John Burrows, an elected

Derbyshire NUM Official, joined a Women's Action Group picket line outside Markham Colliery. He recalled: "The inspector whose name I do not know recognised me and approached. He clearly did not know how best to deal with women's pickets and was awed by how fierce they were. Wanting to insult them and I suspect me, he said 'You don't breed off them cows do you?'

"Yes, but we don't breed pigs like your mothers do." I replied. He was not too happy, cos he expected a thick collier reaction and followed me around for the rest of that night, waiting for a chance to nick me. I was a lot younger then and he couldn't keep up."

Anne Scargill, married to Arthur at the time of the strike, spoke in public many years later about what had happened after her arrest. She had been taken to a police station and "strip-searched", which sounds bad enough. The reality of that experience was much worse because it meant police officers' gloved fingers were poked into body orifices. It was clearly meant to be both painful and humiliating. Anne had told the woman officer who was assaulting her in this way that she should be ashamed of herself. The officer's answer had been to bleat that she was only doing her job. Anne's response?

"That's the excuse the concentration camp guards used – they were only doing their jobs!"

From the way she told her story it was clear Anne had found that episode deeply upsetting, as the police had intended it to be. Yet when they found out how Anne had been treated, many other women were so angry that they too began to picket. Other women were also arrested on picket lines. Toni Bennet from Bolsover, picketing with other Chesterfield Women's Action Group activists, refused to run from a police charge because she said they had done nothing wrong. Innocence was no barrier to arrest, though, as she was then literally dragged away by two police officers, one pulling on each arm. Kate Alvey of Chesterfield said later that Toni had been arrested for singing, which might sound far-fetched unless you had lived in a coalfield that year. The most ridiculous excuses for arrest were invented. One of our members remembered, forty years later, that he had been picketing outside a North Derbyshire coking plant. It was a quiet day, with nothing much happening, so he fished out a pack of cards and started playing patience. A police officer threatened to arrest him, so he asked what he was supposed to have done. The answer was "Gambling in a public place"!

By November 1984 the situation in North Derbyshire was dire, with large numbers of our members back at work. The NUM could not just ignore the tide of members returning to work, but Thatcher's Law meant pickets were not often allowed by the police to approach strikebreaking miners. These were being bussed or walked into work surrounded by large numbers of officers. Discussion of the need for strike action was impossible in those circumstances. In Brimington near Chesterfield, NUM strikers, often supported by coalfield women activists, used to turn out onto the streets to show their anger at strike breakers as one shift ended and another began. On November 16 an NCCL observer, in the village for a shift change, produced a report of events. She saw some heavy policing by Derbyshire police along the route, watching police forcing the crowd of 100 or 150 protesters further into the village. She also spotted three other observers in a little group but they were ordered by police to join the large crowd. The two men observers, slow to respond, were jostled by police, while the woman seemed to go backwards into a hedge, together with a policeman. One of the men observers turned round, was grabbed by police and dragged roughly along the pavement, then pushed into a police van that had suddenly appeared. The second man was also arrested, while the woman was distraught. As one of the arrested men turned out to be leader of the NUS at Felixstowe docks, the other two were probably trade unionists from the same workplace. They had come to present a cheque to the Derbyshire NUM Treasurer, who was very upset by events, as were all the observers.

On that same day striking miner John Walton, a member of Derbyshire NUM Area

Executive, recalls that he approached the senior police officer, pointing out that as Vice-chair of the Parish Council he was concerned about the daily trouble on the streets. He suggested that, as the route from the working miner's home to the pit did not require him to walk through the centre of the village, it would calm the situation if the police stopped parading him unnecessarily through the village, but simply escorted him straight home instead. The officer responded

"I don't care who you are, fuck off!"

Orgreave I realised during May and early June 1984 that something big was being planned. At times I had seen Jim Parker, Mick Clapham and Dave Feickert disappearing into Arthur Scargill's office together. Now Jim, as Arthur's driver, did not usually go to meetings in the office, so I knew something unusual was happening. That something, definitely treated as men's business, and as highly confidential, was apparently a plan for Orgreave coking plant, near Rotherham, although no-one would tell me anything about it. A long-running confrontation between pickets and police there had been simmering, sometimes boiling over, for a while, so a mass picket was being planned. In the last few days running up to June 18, it became clear that Arthur Scargill intended this to be a re-run of the famous Battle of Saltley Gates, Birmingham, during the 1972 miners' strike. In that year there had been a massive turnout by NUM pickets, especially from Yorkshire, together with mass walkouts of workers from the large number of nearby workplaces. The resulting crush had forced the police to order the closure of the coking plant gates. Because that had cut off the supply of coke powering nearby industries, it had been a pivotal moment in the success of the 1972 strike. Twelve years later in1984 Arthur Scargill was hoping for a similar massive turnout so that Orgreave would become the new legendary victory. Unlike Saltley, though, Orgreave was not surrounded by other large workplaces. The only way to get there was by bus or car. Arthur's call was for large numbers of pickets from different coalfields, and from the wider labour movement, on 18 June. I thought this might be a turning point in the strike, but as it was not part of my job to be there, I decided to book a day of annual leave for that Monday and go there in my own time.

Because NEC member Wes Chambers was to oversee the Control Room on the big day, I offered to drive him around the Orgreave area on the previous evening, a Sunday. We had no mobile phones then, so it would be impossible to communicate anything that happened at the picket to those back at National Office. Wes would have to rely on what he saw on the small TV set in the Control Room, or on any landline calls that might come in. As I drove him around the village and past the plant, trying to understand the layout, everything seemed calm in the warm sunlight. It was impossible to imagine the fear I would feel the following day.

Monday morning comes quickly, as I have to be up very early. I put on the pit boots I was given on an underground visit, so if anyone treads on my toes I'll be protected. My long hair is tied back to make it harder for anyone to grab hold of it. In a pair of jeans and a clean white tee-shirt, I think in my innocence that I'm ready for anything. After all, I've taken part in a number of famous demonstrations in the past. In 1968, as the march against the Vietnam war headed for Grosvenor Square, I had seen police behave badly as they picked out a young woman for no apparent reason, then threw her across the road so she skidded painfully on knees and hands. Yet I believe there are some boundaries to police behaviour – a naïve belief that is about to be shattered for ever. At National Office very early, I join some Scottish members whose bus has detoured to collect me by arrangement with one of the branch officials. Before we reach our destination, though, we are stopped by the police.

"Your bus isn't going any further – it stops here. You'll have to walk."

There is no point in arguing.

"We're going to end up a long way from the position we were told to take up by the union" mutters one of the bus leaders. Only then do I begin to realise that the mysterious plan hatched in Arthur Scargill's office was about the precise deployment of different groups of pickets at various sites near to the plant. Later I discover many of the other buses have also been stopped or re-directed by the police. How do they know the ins and outs of the deployment plan? These tactics were created in Arthur Scargill's office in such secrecy that few people at National Office knew anything about it, although at some stage various Area Officials from across the coalfields must have been told at least where their pickets are to go on arrival.

Whatever method the police have used to get hold of the information, once they begin to choose which buses to stop at Orgreave and which to let through, they have wrecked the NUM deployment plan. They are now placing us exactly where they want us. We walk down a field, then stand in a large group of pickets on the sloping public road between the village and the coking works, looking down at the plant. Beyond the front line of pickets is a no-man's land, then huge numbers of police officers, sheltering behind long riot shields, wearing riot helmets with visors pulled down over their faces. It looks and feels very threatening, like the start of a medieval battle with soldiers laid out in formations, except that a battle requires both sides to be armed. Today only one side, the police, has arrived with weapons. That's why I would, in years to come, always reject the term "Battle of Orgreave". Of course we have neither weapons nor protective gear, with most of us just in tee-shirts on this hot summer's day. The only intention of the mass picket is to use large numbers of people to block the way so lorries can no longer ferry coke out to the Scunthorpe steelworks. Occasionally a stone flies over from somewhere behind us, landing among the pickets. After a while Arthur appears with Jim Parker.

"How are things going?" he asks me.

"All right, but someone seems to be throwing stones from behind us at times, and they're landing on us more often than they're clearing the police riot shields".

"We don't want stone-throwing", he calls out.

"See to it" he instructs me, as he turns away with Jim.

Well, thanks, Arthur, I think. What can I do about it? If you don't know who's doing it, how do you persuade them to stop? So of course it doesn't stop, but I don't see it as a big problem. I wonder if the stone-thrower is a police officer posing as a picket, because the occasional missiles are going nowhere near the massed police officers. There are lots of wounded men about, bleeding after military-style advances and assaults by police. Moving about later, I spot a thick-set middle-aged man with black hair, leaning against a stone wall. As he fishes out a large handkerchief he winces in pain, then wipes his face. He almost seems to disbelieve his own words as he mutters "It's class war!" Later I meet Jim Parker for the second time. I can see he's standing and moving stiffly, one hand on his lower back.

"What's the matter, Jim – you don't look so good."

"Well, we were running from 't'orses, an't lad next to me went down. I didn't think they'd 'it me if I bent down to pick someone up, so I stopped to 'elp him – and got a truncheon on mi back!"

Jim has always been gentle and friendly to me and everyone else at National Office, but I think he must be tough when necessary. How else would he have ended up as Arthur's driver? Although the word bodyguard has never been used in my hearing, he is always out and about with Arthur, keeping an eye on him. Later I am approached by a woman I think might be film-maker Yvette Vanson, who has a camerawoman with her. Heading straight towards me she demands

"What's it like being a woman on this picket?"

A feminist since my teenage years, I would normally be pleased to discuss being a woman on a picket line, but today the appalling police behaviour is the only thing on my mind. Expecting a film-maker to be concerned to show how viciously the police are attacking us, I'm utterly thrown by her question. After a few seconds of recovery I say sharply

"The fact that I'm a woman is irrelevant – what matters to me right now is the way we're all being attacked by the police."

She disappears quickly.

The tight police formation, fronted by long riot shields, has gradually pushed our group back up the sloping road across the railway bridge. Every time they advance we move backwards, further and further away from the coking plant. Feeling frustrated, I say

"Look, the police aren't doing anything to us, so why are we retreating all the time?"

The Scottish miner standing next to me says loudly

"Yes, stand your ground!"

So we do. Next time the police push forward we just keep still, then their front row of men with long riot shields parts. Mounted officers come through with very long truncheons drawn, picking up speed. That's the end of standing our ground. Dread propels us into wordless, desperate flight as I feel my fear expanding, filling my chest. We know that trying to run away from the police doesn't count in your favour once they catch you. We've already seen too many men, blood pouring from head wounds, who have been hit by police truncheons, often on the backs of their heads as they try to run away. Although we're running as fast as we can, humans can't outrun horses, so the mounted police are gaining on us. Then one of our group spots a break in the row of terraced houses that follows the line of the road. Using all his breath just to run he can't speak, so instead points to the path leading through the gap. We veer off to the right, running through into the back yards. Here is a huddle of bewildered elderly residents, astounded at what's happening around their own homes. Far from being a safer place, the back yards feel more exposed than the road. In the field beyond the back fences we can see a few pickets running away. Mounted police have galloped past the row of houses, turning at the junction, then riding straight into the field. There they are chasing the fleeing men, clubbing down anyone they can reach. I feel more frightened than ever, and that feeling seems to be shared. Just one house in the row has an open back door. The men in our group are yelling at me

"Get into that house!"

"Go inside, you'll be safer there!"

This doesn't seem to be the moment to try proving that women can be as brave as men. Bowing to group pressure as well as my fear, I dodge through the open back door. Inside, before I've had time to take more than a few panting breaths, a woman appears. With the righteous belligerence of Norah Batty repelling Compo, she demands

"What are you doing inside my house?"

Doesn't she know what's going on outside? Or doesn't she bloody well care? Either way, she clearly isn't going to help me.

Still breathless from our terrified dash to escape the cavalry charge, I try to explain.

"The men told me to come inside, out of the way of the police."

She is unmoved.

I'm sorry, I'll go."

Back outside, I'm met with dismay by the Scottish miners.

"Why did you come back out?"

"It was safer inside, you should've stayed there."

"The woman who lives there doesn't want me in her house, so I had to leave".

Back in the sunshine, things seem even worse. One of the men in the field, truncheoned by a mounted policeman, has scrambled over the fence into the back yards. He's lying on the ground with a bleeding head, surrounded by our group, who are trying to help him although they don't know him. Not one of us has any first aid supplies. Suddenly a squad of foot police in riot gear appears in the backyards, truncheons drawn. One of them, small round shield slung on his left arm, right hand slapping the truncheon into his left palm, is clearly dying to have a go at us. They are right in our faces. One policeman orders us to go back past their squad, onto the road. The idea of passing within inches of their truncheons is one my frightened mind rejects completely. Anyway, we have no idea how far the mounted police line has moved, so going past this aggressive bunch along the alleyway back onto the road could be even more dangerous. Clearly I'm not the only one who doesn't fancy running the gauntlet through a police snatch squad:

"We can't leave him – he's injured."

He is pointing to the man laid out on the ground, head bleeding. Not for a single moment do the police seem to consider calling a first aider to help this wounded man. Instead they see him as they see us: as enemies – or perhaps their prey.

"No, I'm all right now..."

The injured man is bravely trying to struggle up off the ground.

One of our group mutters to him "Shut the fuck up – you're our alibi. Stay down."

In no fit state to challenge that instruction from a fellow-picket, the wounded man sinks back onto the ground.

We can't spin this out much longer. At the next order to go past the police line, we've run out of excuses. As slowly as possible we help the injured miner up and head towards the police snatch squad. I'm dreading what they might do, but the little group of elderly residents seems to save us. Anything the police do will be seen by independent witnesses just a few yards away. As we pass close by the police no blow is struck at us, although I expect one every moment. Once through the alley and back on the road I feel even more vulnerable. As some police horses have passed the alleyway entrance, then halted, we are now sandwiched between the rear ends of the horses and the front of the snatch squad, out of sight of those resident witnesses who have been our saviours. As we can't go back towards the riot squad, with their truncheons still raised, we nervously approach the line of horses from behind, then somehow we are allowed to slip through between them. The police don't seem to want any straggling pickets left behind their front line of horsemen. Later I would learn that we were lucky because other stragglers in our situation were often assaulted then arrested.

By this time some of us are ready for a rest in a calmer atmosphere, so we flop down on a patch of grass outside a little supermarket to rest in the sun. Later, when things are quieter, a couple of us walk back down the hill towards the coking plant. It's like a battlefield, with a police field kitchen still operating in a large tent within the perimeter of the plant. There seems to be a police first aid post, although I neither see nor hear of any injured pickets being treated by police. Some of the dry-stone walls along the side of the road have been knocked down, while every so often I can see the remains of a makeshift barricade, even one fire. Having brought no weapons, the pickets have been forced to improvise protection from the onslaught with whatever materials come to hand.

Eventually we walk back to the bus that will take the Scottish miners home. Once we are seated inside it, the tensions and fears that have built up during the day are coming out in the men's language – the word "fucking" seems to be included every time anyone speaks. One of the branch officials, concerned about this, gets up and speaks to them all.

"Look, we've got a lassie from National Office with us on the bus. I appeal to you to mind your language".

Now I could do without being called a lassie from National Office, but I know that normally miners never swear in front of women. The branch official's appeal fails because events that day, unique in all our lives, have broken down all the usual restraints. These men have seen and felt so much in the last few hours that their emotions are just spilling over.

Once the Scottish miners' bus has dropped me at National Office in central Sheffield, I find a miner sitting on a borrowed chair in the entrance hall. He must have been separated from his mates at Orgreave, but somehow has managed to get back to our office, where assistant receptionist Fran is attending to a bleeding wound on his head. The porter in the foyer of our rented offices is clearly unused to the drama of men with bloody heads staggering into his marble hall. I take the lift to the eighth floor so I can report to Wes Chambers in the Control Room. He goes back to his hotel shortly afterwards. Yes, I know I'm officially on a day's annual leave, but somehow I feel the need to go back on duty that evening, as it wouldn't feel right just to go home with my knowledge of what's happened. My first priority, though, is to have a wash. As I pull off my clothes I notice an unpleasant smell that puzzles me at first. Then I decide that it must be the stench of my own body, generated by the fear I have felt throughout the day. Washed and in the fresh clothes I left in my office early that morning, I feel a bit more ready to deal with the many phone calls that are starting to come through.

"NUM Control Room, Hilary Cave speaking. What can I do to help you?"

It turns out to be an official from another union.

"I don't want to speak to a woman. I want to hear what's been happening from someone who was there."

My annoyance must be coming out in my voice.

"You're speaking to someone who was there – I've only just got back from Orgreave."

Then I answer his questions about what has been going on.

Another call, along similar lines, comes in. This time it's a retired miner, clearly upset at what he's seen on TV.

After I introduce myself:

"I don't want to talk to a girl, I want to talk to a man who was there".

Somehow, knowing he's a miner, I muster more patience. We have a long talk, both shedding a few tears. He can hardly believe what he's seen on television news.

"I never thought I'd see it happening in our own country – men being run down by police horses" he says wonderingly as we finish our discussion.

Over time I found out more about other pickets' experiences on June 18. Dennis Clayton was one of a group from Bolsover Colliery who arrived at Orgreave in several cars.

"We'd been to Orgeave before, but that day were different – there were signs saying "Orgreave this way". We ended up right outside the coking plant gate, close to some Scottish lads. There was a big shove. Police and horses charged so we ended up by a supermarket. We went up a gennel (alley) between some houses, and an old lady invited us into her front room. We were choc-a-bloc, a dozen of us in her front room, panting, arms up in the air because there was no space. Everybody stank because we'd been too busy picketing to have baths. We were there about twenty-five minutes. Then we came out of the house and back to the main gates. Everybody was scattered."

Nobody in his group was hurt that day, thanks to the kindness of the elderly woman who sheltered them. Dennis and his mates must have been only yards from my group as we fled from the police horses and their truncheon-wielding riders. At that point we had no idea some others had been offered safe haven inside a house.

George Bell from Shireoaks Colliery had another worry on top of fear for his safety as he ran from the cavalry charge on June 18th. Living under bail restrictions because he had been arrested earlier in the strike for allegedly obstructing a police officer, he could not afford to get arrested again. Even a small fine would probably have cost him his job, as hundreds of miners were finding out. George ran into the supermarket, but as police officers were still chasing, he dived flat under a display of beans and soups. He could hear staff shouting in surprise as a police horse apparently appeared in the entrance, so stayed hidden until it was safe.

John Walton from Ireland colliery in Derbyshire had been to Orgreave several times before, often as one of a small number of pickets halted by police roadblocks. On that Monday everything was different. There were large numbers of pickets, with John's group directed in by some of the thousands of police officers, so ending up exactly where the police wanted them. Another picket advised John that if there was a charge by mounted police it was safer to climb onto the roadside wall so the horses would just move past him. When John did this

"I was pushed off the wall by a poke from a copper's truncheon as the horses rushed past us. He knocked me off the wall and then I couldn't breathe. Some lads from Northumberland helped me and took me in their car to Chesterfield Royal Hospital. Although the police had a field hospital, with police first aiders roaming about, I never saw them give any help to injured pickets. When I got to the hospital there were lots of injured lads there who'd come from Orgreave".

John Walton's verdict on that day at Orgreave was: "The police had come to make war on us – and they enjoyed it!"

On June 18 itself, I believed that police behaviour had simply run out of control but as I have interviewed people, discussed events of that day, and read other assessments, I now believe that their behaviour was planned well in advance. They had visited the plant well before the strike began to inform management about new policing arrangements. ACPO had created and began to use a new police manual "Public Order and Tactical Options". Apparently borrowing from previous police practices in the British Empire, it called for paramilitary practices such as short shield officers running into crowds with batons drawn to create fear and possibly injury. I remember the fear I felt when they did that to us, although we were not a crowd, just a small group of men and one woman dressed in jeans and tee-shirts, without weapons or defensive gear. Solicitor Gareth Peirce, who represented some of our members on 18 June, has pointed out that some of the practices set out in the manual were illegal. The police were using the National Reporting Centre, which was in fact a national officer deployment machine that broke the rule about supposed independence of separate constabularies. That machinery, used regularly during the strike, reached its pinnacle at Orgreave on June 18, although police had been ratcheting up tension at Orgreave for some time.

Police tactics at Orgreave on that day suggest they had made detailed plans beforehand, with huge numbers of officers present. They apparently cleared pickets from the field, which was private property, pushing everyone onto the road. Yet pickets standing in a field have no hope of stopping lorries carrying coke on a public road, so why would the police want to move them onto the road, where there was a chance that the crowd might stop lorries? Next they pushed us back up the road, away from the coking plant and into the village. Some of our defendants at the subsequent trial, following discussions with lawyers, were advised that riot charges against them could only be sustained if they were in a public place such as the village, rather than in a privately-owned field. Bearing in mind the evidence of a Cabinet decision about riot charges arising from the Mansfield rally a month before June 18, it seems reasonable to conclude that Cabinet had also reached a decision before June 18 that riot charges would be brought against pickets at Orgreave on that day. The experience of Robert Plant, a Derbyshire miner, supports the idea of thorough police pre-planning. Arrested on the field, assaulted by more than one officer, Robert was placed in a holding area in a building prepared for that purpose. He thought it had been a first aid building for the coking plant, which suggests that co-operation by plant management had either been requested or ordered by the police. Inside that building he saw a picket who had been beaten up, together with about forty people, both police and arrested men.

Thatcher's Law dealt efficiently with events at Orgreave on June 18. The Government propaganda machine, assisted by its willing media accomplices, went into overdrive. Many of our members, arrested and often assaulted by the police onslaught, sometimes denied the hospital treatment they required, found themselves cast as violent rioters rather than victims of police violence. Within hours Arthur Scargill rang our Control Room, apparently from his hospital bed, telling me that one of our members was so badly injured that he was on a life-support machine. A red-haired picket appeared on BBC TV news as he was being beaten around the head by a police officer wielding a truncheon. That sequence was ended very quickly, presumably because it did not fit the official narrative of violent miners attacking police. I have been told by someone who recently saw the unedited footage that the police officer broke his truncheon on that picket's head. Only many years later did the BBC admit to "an accidental reversal of film footage" on June 18,1984 news. Such reversals gave an entirely false picture of events, making defensive actions appear to have been offensive.

With the huge number of arrests at Orgreave, many of our members spent the night in prison cells awaiting their Court appearances, so missing their NUM-chartered buses home. As striking miners hardly ever had cash in their pockets, we could not just abandon them on the streets of Rotherham once they left the courthouse, so I volunteered to drive over from Sheffield carrying a large bag of cash to pay their fares home. Once I had found the Magistrates' Court it was easy to spot our members, who looked weary and shaken, sometimes blood-stained and stitched, as they came out of the building.

"Hello, I'm Hilary from National Office. Are you NUM? I can give you money to get home if you tell me where you're from."

Then I would search the sheet from Finance section, showing rough costs for fares to the various coalfields. I was alternately kneeling then crouching, depending on whether hips or knees were hurting most, on the pavement outside the Rotherham Magistrates' Court. As I counted out onto the pavement what was needed by each man, I was vaguely aware that this must be a comic scene to passers-by. Without so much as a picnic table to sit at while I was doing the job, though, the pavement was my only available resource. Good job it's summer, I thought – at least there's no snow!

While handing out the money I had identified a few miners who needed to get to Sheffield to catch trains home, so I offered a lift to as many as I could squeeze into my car. During the drive back to the station it became clear that they were all worn out after a night in the cells, while some were injured. I asked if anybody wanted to stay the night at my house to rest before they caught the train home. The two youngest-looking miners accepted the offer, so after dropping the others at the station I turned in my seat and looked at the pair.

"My name's Hilary – I'm sorry I haven't picked up your names yet."

The taller, heavier dark-haired lad said he was Craig, while the wiry light-haired young man was Eric. They were good friends, I believe from Oakley, a Scottish mining village with a militant reputation. As I saw some of Eric's wounds and his bloodstained clothes I began to feel queasy.

"What happened, Eric? You don't look so well."

"We were running from the police horses and we couldn't get away fast enough. They caught me... In the end, they took me to hospital. The nurse stitched me up and told them I wasn't well enough to go back to the police station. They took no notice of her and carted me back to the cells, then to court today."

"Well, let's go back to National Office and get you both a hot drink, then I can take you to my house and you can have a rest, a shower and something to eat."

As I made them a drink at the office I began to worry that perhaps Eric ought to see a doctor to get his head wound checked. The trouble was that feelings were so polarised, especially after misleading BBC TV coverage the previous day, that I could not guarantee Eric would get an appropriate response from a doctor. Someone said there was a sympathetic GP at Parson's Cross, on the north side of the city, so I drove the three of us there. Apparently the doctor thought Eric was OK – or so Eric said.

After the long drive back to my terraced house in Chesterfield, I made some food while the young men took showers. Eric was in such difficulty that Craig had to help him. While I was wishing I had some clean men's clothes for them to climb into, instead of the clothes that they'd worn constantly since Sunday night, Craig stuck his head through the doorway of my little kitchen.

"I think you ought to come and have a look at Eric."

I followed him upstairs to the bathroom, where Eric had put his grubby jeans back on.

"Let Hilary see your back."

It was now clear that Eric's knuckle, elbow and the back of his head had all been cut and stitched. His hand and elbow looked swollen, too, around the cuts. As he turned his back towards me I could see a bruise just the shape and size of the long truncheons used by mounted police. After that first moment of shock, I realised we needed to get his injuries on record because they were proof that he had been assaulted from behind.

The following morning we went to National Office before I took them to catch their train home. I introduced Eric to Maurice Jones, editor of The Miner, who could get hold of a photographer quickly. The injuries were photographed in the hope that Eric's NUM-financed solicitor could make use of those images at some time in the future. Later I was told that Gareth Peirce, one of the solicitors representing our members arrested at Orgreave, had been so shocked by their injuries that when she went back home afterwards she had been sick. Apparently she had been particularly worried about the condition of Eric and of Arthur Critchlow, who had been put back into a police cell that night although police had fractured his skull with a truncheon blow to the back of his head.

Not content with assaulting and arresting large numbers of pickets on June 18, the police at that time had powers to decide whether to charge their victims, what those charges would be, and to engage barristers to prosecute defendants in court. Charges of riot, put to defendants such as the badly wounded Arthur Critchlow only many hours after he had been charged with a lesser offence, could carry a life sentence at that time. Others, charged with lesser offences such as affray, could still be facing many years inside. Of varying ages, some with wives and children, our defendants had been forced to endure the appalling strain of such charges for many months because the first group trial was not held until the summer of 1985. They were only the first batch of those charged, with many others still awaiting a later trial date. As we had all known of innocent miners found guilty by the courts during the strike, it would have been naive to expect "Not Guilty" verdicts to be handed down just because the men were innocent. I felt that trial was particularly painful for those of us who had been at Orgreave on June 18 because we knew that chance had determined who had been arrested, and often assaulted, by police. We never discussed that, though. I felt a sort of survivor's guilt. How had I escaped uninjured, while others had been assaulted and then put on trial for riot? Orgreave and the trial that followed were Thatcher's Law in operation: the full weight of state power wielded to crush those who had simply been trying to save their jobs and communities.

So many police officers' statements had used identical language in their statements that the prosecution evidence was becoming less and less credible when tested in court. As the trial had progressed I gathered that Mike Mansfield, one of our NUM defence barristers, had cross-examined one police officer in great detail, drawing contradictory answers on different days. Mike had intended to ask which of the officer's statements was the lie, as both could not be true. Before our barrister could pose that question, though, the state admitted defeat. It seems that the lawyers hired to prosecute our members had seen the weaknesses in their own case. Prosecuting counsel produced a doctor's note to say that the police officer due for cross-examination that day was too ill to testify and would be unfit to do so in the foreseeable future. As soon as I heard this news from Keith Brookes of our Industrial Relations Department, I had the mischievous thought that the officer's incapacitating illness must be perjury. Of course, it would not have been given that name on the medical certificate. Prosecutors declared they would offer no further evidence so the trial was abandoned, leaving Mike Mansfield to add one more to his list of famous victories.

There was tremendous relief when the phone call came through to tell us the trial had collapsed, Everyone from National Office was invited to a snap celebration party that evening at the hotel in Sheffield where defendants were staying, although only those of us without family commitments were able to turn up. The weather was so glorious that occasionally the party spilled outside for photographs. It was there I spotted defendants Eric and Craig, who had stayed overnight with me when they were let out of police cells after their court appearance. Somehow we seemed a bit shy of each other now that the drama of their imprisonment and Eric's injuries had passed. Yet still I could not rid myself of that haunting sense of survivor's guilt.

Back inside, it was story time.

"Come on, Mike, give us the one about the snowman and the Inspector!"

Climbing onto the table so we could all see and hear, Mike Mansfield had to bend his head forward because the ceiling was too low to clear his tall form. As his skilful barrister's delivery mined the tale for all its humour, I realised that although it was clearly a favourite amongst the Yorkshire miners in particular, this story was new to me. Mike told us that pickets at a South Yorkshire pit had been keeping themselves warm and occupied by building an elaborate snowman. Someone had produced a toy policeman's helmet for its head, to the amusement of the pickets, if not of the policemen who had been hanging around with nothing much to do. Then a visiting police inspector had felt the need to exert his authority.

"Clear that snowman away – now!" he had instructed. Suddenly all movement by the pickets had stopped.

"I don't mean tomorrow!" he had snapped. Not a picket had moved.

Determined to overcome this disobedience, the inspector had climbed into the police Land Rover, revved the engine and driven hard at the snowman.

"Such a pity", Mike ended, his voice full of mock regret.

"The snowman had been built around a concrete bollard, so all the Inspector managed to do was write off his new police Land Rover!"

The room erupted with laughter: it wasn't often that our side won anything, so even small victories were treasured and re-told. Of course a much bigger victory was the collapse of the Orgreave trial, but the long ordeal had taken a terrible toll on our defendants. Beneath the laughter and relief that night lay residues of anxiety and fear. Was it over at last? Would they really be able to go home the next day without the threat of life imprisonment hanging over them? The first Orgreave riot trial involved only a small number of those accused of riot, so many more accused men, such as Kevin Horne, had been expecting an even longer wait for their court appearances. Kevin remembers

"It was always hanging over you".

Their knowledge that the huge expense of their solicitors and barristers was being paid by the NUM could never make up for those months of suffering by our defendant miners and their families. Kevin Horne was so traumatised by his experiences that years later, when NUM lawyers were preparing to sue the police for assaults on, and false arrests of, our members arrested on June 18, he refused to take part. He just could not face re-living his experiences in court, even though he would have won some compensation. Kevin's trauma persists, as he still wakes up sometimes thinking about Orgreave and the trial.

The wheels of justice It might be more accurate to describe the legal system, as used against our members during the strike, as the wheels of injustice. At first we were all staggered by the enormity of the terrible misuse of the law and miscarriages of justice, large and small, that were being imposed on our communities, but after a while the utterly ruthless nature of the state became clear to many in our coalfield communities.

As well as the travesties of the justice system at Mansfield and Orgreave riot trials, there were injustices in more minor court hearings. In South Yorkshire's Kiveton Miners' Welfare, a miner's wife explained what had happened at her husband's appearance in Magistrates' Court. Just before he entered the dock, the police had added a second charge to his existing alleged offence. His lawyer asked for an adjournment because there had been no time to prepare a defence for the second charge, but as the Clerk to the Court stated that there was a charge to answer, the magistrates continued. By this point in her story the wife was in tears, overcome by the gross injustice she had witnessed against her husband, describing the magistrates as "sheep". She found that injustice hard to stomach, as it destroyed her belief in the impartiality of the legal system. Many of our members, together with their families, were forced by their experiences to change their views on the way in which the state operated.

Across all British coalfields 11,312 people were arrested in connection with the strike, 7000 were injured, 5600 were put on trial and 200 imprisoned. Striking Notts miner John Dobb summed up the situation perfectly by saying

"When you're up against the state nothing's off the table for them."

The major riot trials following Orgreave and Mansfield were perfect examples of this. Research student Joe Diviney, searching Cabinet Papers of that time, has established that Cabinet discussed on May 17, 1984, what charges should be brought against defendants in the Mansfield riot trial. It was unconstitutional for Cabinet to interfere in the judicial process in that way. Those Cabinet Papers show that although some Ministers were doubtful about whether riot and affray charges should be brought, the Home Secretary was defending their use. Joe Diviney points out that the quality of police evidence can be judged from the fact that by August 15, 1985, even before the prosecution had finished presenting its case against the Mansfield defendants, the judge had already directed the jury to acquit eight of them. The trial ran out of steam, with all remaining Mansfield riot charges being dropped in early October.

It seems likely that Cabinet was also involved in discussing what charges should be brought against the Orgreave defendants. As the trial of the first batch of 18 Orgreave defendants began, on June 10, 1985, they had been waiting under intolerable pressure for a year to see whether they would be given life sentences, which could happen at that time to anyone convicted of riot. Supporting evidence for Government involvement in charging decisions is suggested by the experience of Arthur Critchlow, whose skull had been fractured by a police truncheon on June 18 at Orgreave, but who was not even allowed to stay in hospital overnight. Police insisted on returning him to one of their cells. Arthur said that the charge of riot was made to him at the police station very late on June 18, after he had already been charged with a lesser offence. Following the collapse of the Orgreave trial, it took years before NUM solicitors were able to extract from South Yorkshire Police any compensation for assaults and wrongful arrests. Although thirty-nine miners were awarded a total of £100,000 in legal costs, with £425,000 in compensation in an out of court settlement, South Yorkshire Police never admitted liability. No apology was given by police, no police officers were disciplined for misconduct at Orgreave. Neither were any police officers disciplined over their evidence at the trial, which appeared perjured. Much later, some officers stated publicly that parts of their evidence had been dictated to them by other officers.

Many years later Home Secretary Theresa May led Orgreave Truth and Justice campaigners to believe there would be an official inquiry into police behaviour at Orgreave on June 18, 1984, but once she became Prime Minister, the next Home Secretary Amber Rudd refused to set up such an inquiry. The Orgreave Truth and Justice Campaign is still battling on bravely, with some success. The 2024 Labour Party manifesto promised an investigation or enquiry so that the truth about events at Orgreave comes to light. In my view we need to keep campaigning for the entire strike policing operation in 1984-85 to be investigated, as the police behaved very badly on other occasions too.

Although huge numbers of our members suffered at the hands of the justice system, at least some of those who were helping out the state, while making huge sums of money, seemed to have an easy ride in the courts. Coal Board transport manager Jack Smith recalls that one firm, which made a fortune shifting scab coal during the strike, had committed more than a thousand misdemeanours. Some of their drivers were unlicensed, some were incorrectly licensed, some vehicles had been found on inspection to be unfit for use, some were overloaded, or their drivers had driven for too many hours without a break. When the owners appeared in court the case was simply dismissed by the judge. Jack could not help but compare the behaviour of that firm with Coal Board transport operations, whose managers always complied fully with the law.

Although the state looked the other way when private companies made a fortune out of the strike while breaking the law, their treatment of our union was very different. Court action, instigated originally by Thatcher's deniable asset David Hart, led to the imposition of a Receiver late in 1984. That had a dramatic effect on the way our union operated, as we were no longer allowed access to our own funds. From then on we were paid in cash folded into brown envelopes. The source of that cash was not disclosed but seemed to be other unions, so eventually it would have to be repaid. Any union loaning us money in this way, and indeed any union offering us meaningful solidarity, was liable to find itself with legal problems. Michael Arnold the Receiver, who publicly declared "I am the NUM", was paid huge fees, although we could never quite understand what benefits our members were supposed to be receiving from the period when he was allegedly in charge of our union. Our members' contributions were also paying his expenses. I was told he was staying at the luxury Cavendish Arms hotel in Baslow, a Peak District village, despite the large selection of comfortable hotels available close to our National Office in Sheffield. He seemed to travel to our office in a taxi. I found it hard to stomach the knowledge that he was living such a comfortable life, paid for by our members' money, when most of our members were in extreme hardship during and after the strike.

National Officials made it clear that Finance staff must co-operate with the Receiver. This was not easy for staff, because on top of everything else Michael Arnold behaved in an overbearing way. Our cashier told me that when Arnold arrived in their office he took off his velvet-collared overcoat and handed it to her, as though she were a servant. Although the coatrack was only feet away he clearly had no intention of making the effort to hang up his coat himself. For all his arrogance, Arnold's position as Receiver was simply another of the chains by which the state was trying to bind us. Taken together, they made life difficult for all of us, inflicting great hardship on our striking members.

A tale for snap-time: The Court Usher's tale A long time after the strike, as my partner and I were enjoying a pub lunch, a woman at the next table started to chat to us. Once she knew of our connection to the NUM she told us about the day some miners appeared in Chesterfield Magistrates' Court, where she was Usher. The accused miners had brought along a big group of supporters that she feared might be rowdy, so before the hearing began she walked up to the group and told them sternly that they must behave respectfully and stand up when the magistrates entered.

"All right, Missus, we know you're just doing your job. We'll behave."

Even so, she kept an eye on them when the magistrates came in. Annoyed to see one of the miners still sitting down, she glared at him across the courtroom, calling out

"That means you as well!"

A small voice came back

"I am standing, Missus, it's just that I'm little!"

We laughed, then realised immediately that we knew who she was talking about: a very small miner called Terry who worked at Bolsover. We had seen him regularly in Chesterfield Labour Club with his best mate, who was unusually tall.

8 Making the strike bite

Getting organised By the time of the April 1984 Delegate Conference some Areas, already on strike, had put into place their usual strike arrangements. Once Conference had agreed to support the strike, which was technically a series of Area strikes, nationally approved, similar arrangements were made across all the coalfields. It was more difficult in Notts, where many branch officials were not on strike, so strikers lacked union offices and other resources, as well as sometimes lacking experience of organising a strike. John Dobb of Bottom Pit at Hucknall remembers one of the leading Yorkshire full-time officials came down to a meeting, offering valuable advice on organisation. Local strike centres, often based in Miners' Welfare buildings, would operate round the clock, acting as rapid communication links between Area officials, branch officials and the membership. At local strike centres it was usually a branch official who sorted out the deployment of pickets, with small payments made to each member who did picket duty. Sometimes Thatcher's Law meant that such branch officials were arrested, then forbidden by bail conditions to go near Coal Board premises for months on end. When that happened to Snowy Bradley, NUM branch secretary at Arkwright colliery near Chesterfield, he handed over the job of picket organisation to Steve Brunt. Some of our members banned in that way from picketing simply carried on as before, but in doing so risked further legal and employment penalties.

Cars were often needed to ferry strikers to picket lines and to shift the large quantities of food needed for communal kitchens or weekly food parcels. As striking miners had no money to pay garage bills, other ways had to be found to keep their vehicles running. Some of our members from Duckmanton Coal Board Workshops near Chesterfield used their mechanical expertise to set up a car maintenance and repair squad. Several North Derbyshire strikers, unwilling to join picket lines but still keen to make their contribution, found a home in that group.

As it quickly became clear that police would single out for attack any of our pickets who were tall and well-built, members such as Ian Street from Duckmanton Workshops often wisely opted for other duties. Because Government, following the Ridley Plan, had altered benefits system rules to punish strikers, it was important to understand the system in order to extract every possible penny of the miserly benefits that could be claimed. Ian Street received training in Welfare Rights, probably with the help of the local Unemployed Workers' Centre and Derbyshire County Council, so for the next year he ran advice sessions in the strike centre that had been set up in the Chesterfield Labour Club just across the road from the NUM Area Offices. As the Club had been revitalised by the recent election of Tony Benn as MP for Chesterfield, it played a valuable role throughout the strike, with Tony regularly visiting to find out what problems were being experienced by our members and their families. At Shireoaks pit in Bassetlaw Glyn Gilfoyle also undertook training from various sources so he could offer advice about benefits and money to their members.

Striking workers received nothing at all for themselves, so single miners rapidly fell into dire poverty, having to rely on family and friends for the most basic supplies. Arthur Scargill told a story about a single man, living a long way from any help at a strike centre, whose jeans had worn into rags over the first few months of the strike because he had no income. Once he managed to find a strike centre he was able to access food, while the women searched their stockpile of donated clothes until they found jeans that would fit him. When at work, Coal Board employees received a coal allowance but that ceased as soon as strike action began. The result was freezing homes and no water for hot showers, so our striking members and families were cold, hungry and short of clothes.

NUM Areas worked hard to win grassroots solidarity, dispatching fund-raisers to various towns and cities outside the coalfields. There were some tensions at first if miners from more than one NUM Area had gone to the same city, but this was sorted out very quickly once the various Area officials had met and agreed on territorial boundaries. Ken Evans was Kent Area's representative in London. He had stayed with some friends of mine for months, collecting money in the street during the day, often speaking at labour movement meetings to win support in the evenings. They invited him to stay over the Christmas holiday, when I joined them for a few days. With the time for Christmas dinner approaching, Ken became very unwell with chest pain. As he was to be taken to hospital in an ambulance I offered to go with him so the others could enjoy their Christmas dinner without interruption. At Middlesex Hospital the doctor wanted to know who I was. In response to her question, we assured her we were neither married nor partnered, but just friends. Even the term "friends" was stretching it a bit, as we'd only known each other for a couple of days, but no other suitable answer came to mind. Once the doctor had finished inquiring into our relationship she turned her attention to Ken's health – and about time, too, I thought. He told her about a heart condition, admitting he had failed to take his medication recently. Unimpressed, she asked why.

"Well, as a striking miner the only money I have is what I can collect in London and it doesn't seem right to spend it on myself. I send it all back to Kent for the hardship fund."

I was shocked.

"But Ken, nobody would object to you spending some of that money on your prescription. We need you to be as well as possible because we need your work for the union in London. Please, promise me you'll take your tablets from now on."

Although he made that promise I was not convinced he would keep it. After a few hours he was discharged so I called a cab to get us back to Harlesden for some warmed-up Christmas dinner. Ken carried on with his fund-raising in London.

Striking women Although press and television often portrayed our striking members as macho men, intimidating others, some of our women members also mounted brave strike action. Some canteen workers, almost always women, went on strike, although canteen workers in Yorkshire had sometimes in the recent past been discouraged from joining in everyday branch activities. Our COSA section for white-collar workers organised some clerical workers, including women, in the coal industry, while APEX organised others. APEX, a separate union from the NUM, was never part of the strike action in 1984-5. At least three quarters of the Coal Board Pensions and Insurance Department, based in an office near ours in Sheffield, were women. Some of those workers were employed on short-term contracts, which always leaves employees more vulnerable to management pressure. Despite that, the new COSA branch leadership at Pensions and Insurance, including a woman, worked hard to get their members involved in the overtime ban. Some of us at National Office would occasionally join them on their Saturday morning picket, while they had support from miners at High Moor and a meeting addressed by Arthur. Once the strike began, though, the situation became much more difficult for them, with a woman branch officer believing that COSA national leader Trevor Bell was pretending to support the strike while really trying to undermine it. Always a right-winger, he had challenged Arthur Scargill in an election for the post of National President. While visiting some local training workshops after the strike I was startled and annoyed to hear one of our members dismissing canteen workers at his colliery, who had not joined the strike, as "cows". My reply was extremely sharp as I challenged him about how hard they had tried to persuade the canteen women to join the strike, while telling him off for referring to fellow-members of our union in that way.

Trying to keep up morale in Notts Some of us at National Office had our own personal contacts in various coalfields. I knew miners in Clay Cross and Chesterfield, where I had lived and worked for many years, as well as knowing miners in Hucknall and Linby, South Notts, where my comrade and partner Barry Johnson lived. Because they lacked support from their own branch officials the loyal strikers, always keen to have speakers from the national union, would sometimes ask me to speak at their Sunday morning meetings held in the upstairs room of the Plough at Hucknall. As there were only 44 strikers out of 1000 workers at Hucknall's Bottom Pit, they suffered a lot of social pressure from scabs. Also suffering great financial hardship, strikers in Notts were always hungry for news and support. I would try to bring news of developments, although as time went on there was little, then no, good news to bring. Years later, striker Jim McDowall grumbled

"You always said the same thing – what a good job we were doing, and we should carry on".

Sorry, Jim, I couldn't think of anything else to say.

A tale for snap time: The Tease I had seen the strident headlines and the photo of our Chief Executive, Roger Windsor, kissing Colonel Gaddafi, apparently somewhere in Libya. Up and down the country readers had devoured, along with their Sunday cornflakes, an angry article accusing the union of toadying to Gaddafi in order to beg money from him for our strike funds. My immediate guess had been that Roger had probably been dispatched to Libya for the opposite reason – an attempt to put the NUM's money where the British Government and courts could not lay hands on it. Whatever the reason for his trip, it was bad publicity for our Chief Executive to be seen kissing the man described by the British press as the world's most monstrous leader. A number of us were talking about this in the office kitchen before work the following morning. Once Roger himself walked in I couldn't resist a tease.

"That must be the second most famous kiss in history, Roger".

Obviously annoyed, he glared, then silenced me with a single dismissive sentence.

"Last time I saw you, you were undressed".

He walked out of the kitchen, leaving me facing my workmates, with the room in startled silence. I was unable to deny what he'd said. Even worse, I couldn't think of a single useful word to utter. How had I got myself into this pickle? Let me explain...

It had started a few days previously, when I had been on night duty. Throughout the strike some senior officers took it in turns to stay in the building overnight, alone on duty in what was called the Control Room – a Scargillian aspiration rather than a reality, as each NUM Area had its own headquarters, with local Strike Centres usually based in Miners' Welfares. It was at the Strike Centres, and possibly Area offices, where day-to-day decisions were made about picketing and strike organisation. In the National Office Control Room, then, we would deal with anything that cropped up out of office hours, although such issues were rarely urgent. As our night shifts followed a normal day's work, then a lonely evening shift, I always felt in need of a rest by midnight. Ever hopeful, I would change into a nightdress and settle onto the grubby camp bed.

The evening had followed the usual pattern: my short sleep had been interrupted by that bloody phone again. Through the fog of fatigue, it had taken me a while to grasp that the caller was Nell Myers, Arthur Scargill's PA, who lived mainly in London. Why was she ringing me at this time of night? She said she was in the building, ringing from the porter's phone in the entrance hall downstairs, because she had just locked herself out of the office by accident. At night we needed two keys, one to get us into or out of the building, the second to get us from the stairwell and toilet area into our offices on the top floors. Why on earth hadn't Nell let me know she was in the building before, when I'd thought I was alone? Still groggy, I grabbed my key and went into the stairwell to rescue her. As soon as the door shut behind me I realised, with a lurch to my stomach, that instead of picking up the key for the door between stairwell and office, I was clutching the key to the downstairs outside door. Now we were both trapped in the stairwell, and all I was wearing was a nightdress. Staring at this wrong key in my hand, I cursed my stupidity. Anger directed at myself was useless, though. First I needed to join Nell, so I tripped the heavy fantastic in cold bare feet down seven flights of polished marble chip staircase. We avoided the lift at night because, without a night porter, there was no hope of rescue if it went wrong.

It was never clear to me how Nell had been so badly-organised that she got locked out, yet so well-organised that she had her bag containing her phone book on her shoulder. My only resources were an absence of proper clothes and the wrong key. As our options were limited to standing in the bare marble entrance hall all night or summoning help, we agreed to ring someone. Which unlucky colleague would we try to drag out of bed at that hour? Nell said that Roger lived closer than anyone else, so she rang him from the porter's phone. As it would be a while before he could get dressed and drive over, Nell encouraged me to try to sleep again.

The only hope of sleep was a barefoot climb back up to the seventh floor so I could bed down in the corridor outside Reception. Resting my head on a pile of second-hand clothes donated for striking miners' families, sleep must have come quickly. My next memory is of Roger and Nell standing over me, saying we could now get back into the office. I must have been a comical sight, stumbling to my feet from a pile of old clothes, nightdress askew. We both thanked Roger with feeling, although I had not anticipated that the following morning I would have to pay publicly for our rescue by being embarrassed in front of my colleagues. That taught me never to tease Roger again.

South Wales pickets in Hucknall
The Nottinghamshire strikers named themselves "Loyal to the Last" – and they were. Their numbers, though, were too small to cover all the coalfield's picketing needs, so South Wales NUM offered, or was asked, to supply some pickets to help them out. (Single stop only) They would need to travel discreetly, so as not to be stopped at the motorway roadblocks as they travelled into Notts. They would also need accommodation. Somehow arrangements were made without giving away vital information on the phones. Barry Johnson, President of Chesterfield Trades Council, and a Hucknall resident who regularly picketed at Linby, had promised to find billets for these South Wales men. He would take in some, his brother would take in a group, while others were to be placed in different homes around the town. So as not to alert the police, the pickets would travel up on Sunday, sharing several cars. Barry and I needed to find them and

get them away quickly once they arrived in Hucknall, to avoid alerting the police at the town's Divisional Police Headquarters a few hundred yards away. In miserable winter dusk we drove to the Market Place then separated, each wandering up and down the main street in search of groups of men who looked a bit lost. It was easy to spot them because the main street was almost deserted. I crossed the road to speak to a likely-looking group.

"Excuse me, are you NUM?"

They nodded. I needed to make sure, though. Who knew whether our messages had been intercepted?

"From South Wales?"

"That's right, love."

"I'm Hilary Cave, the Union's National Education Officer. Thanks very much for coming – things are very difficult in Notts, so we really appreciate your support. I've got connections here, so I can show you where you'll be staying."

"We're glad to see you. We've been wandering about for ten minutes and were starting to worry nobody was going to pick us up."

Barry was further down the street, talking to another little group. He would take them to his brother's house on the other side of town. When I took the South Wales men to Barry's house I offered them some food, but nobody seemed to be hungry. I wondered if they had just got used to living on very little food. Once Barry joined us at his house, we explained to the visitors that we were short of beds, but would share out what bedding we could. Our guests seemed very adaptable, with one choosing to sleep on the sofa, one on the floor and one taking the last bit of floor space under the table. What surprised us most was that one of them chose to sleep on the staircase, where he said he felt most comfortable. I showed them how to access the breakfast things and the bathroom, then we all had an early night. By the time I went downstairs the following morning to get ready for my long drive to Sheffield they had already left for an early picket. I don't think I ever managed to grasp their names – we knew them, yet didn't know them. It was enough for us, and them, that we were struggling for the same cause.

The Control Room at National Office "Just what did you think you were doing? What right have you got to be telling my members in our strike centre what to do?"

Although he was ringing from Barnsley, the voice of the Yorkshire Miners' President seemed to echo around the Control Room in Sheffield as loudly as if he were standing next to me, addressing a rally. Trying to suppress a sigh, I knew I needed to calm him down before he would be ready to listen to my side of the discussion I'd had on the phone with a miner at one of the Yorkshire Strike Centres.

"I think there's been some misunderstanding, Jack".

Trying for a soothing tone, I went on

"I was asking, not telling. You see, I've had a call from the leader of a group of COSA (the white-collar section of the union) pickets who've been stuck at Connah's Quay power station since yesterday. He said they've had no food, drink, or shelter since they arrived and he's pleading with me to find some new pickets to relieve them as soon as possible. Of course I promised to do my best. Given how far away Connah's Quay is, even if a new team set off straight away it would take hours to reach them. So all I was doing was pleading for help from your strike centre so we can relieve those pickets who need help at Connah's Quay. I wouldn't dream of trying to tell your members what to do – I was just asking for help."

As I carried on in this vein he began to calm down bit by bit, finally agreeing that they would send some pickets to relieve the men stranded miles from any food or drink. Duties in the Control Room could be very tricky, trapped in the fault-lines between competing power bases at National and Area Offices. These power struggles arose from the NUM's federal structure, with each Area being a union in its own right, employing its own staff and owning its own property. Area Officials could be very prickly if they thought National was interfering in Area business. As deployment of pickets was undoubtedly Area business, National Office had to ask, not instruct. Yet even when we asked, it was sometimes seen as ordering. So, except in Arthur Scargill's dreams, the Control Room never controlled anything significant. Yet it played a valuable part in liaison between Areas and National Office, while absorbing tremendous amounts of National Office staff time and energy for twenty-four-hour cover, seven days a week throughout the year of the strike.

The first Control Room night shift was covered by Trevor Cave, Head of Administration, paired with Margaret Fellowes, who supervised the secretaries. Supported by his book and her knitting, they tried to stay awake all night, combating their drowsiness by polite conversation and regular cups of tea. After that experience it was quickly decided to slash night cover to a single person. Because we had always done our normal day's work in the office before starting a night shift, it quickly became clear that we needed a camp bed. Someone produced one with some sort of blanket and a thin, lumpy pillow, although as time went on it became clear that I was the only person who ever supplied a clean pillow-case. Could that have been because all the other camp-bed users were men? Still, the bed was a vast improvement, so when my turn for night-duty came I always hoped for a few hours' sleep at least. As I lived in Chesterfield I could afford neither the time nor the money to drive home between day and night shifts, so when my turn came I usually did my day's work, then an evening shift, then a night shift all in one go. There was little chance of sleep, though, on Control Room duty. Somehow late-night beer seemed to sharpen people's generosity, so they would ring at strange hours requesting details of the Miners' Solidarity Fund in order to make donations.

One late-night caller had intentions that were the opposite of generous. After what seemed only a few minutes of sleep the phone pierced my rest again. Rolling off the camp bed, catching myself on its frame, I reached for the disrupting phone.

"Hello is that the NUM?"

Having been deeply asleep, but for too short a time, somehow my tongue had not quite remembered how to form the words, but I was trying hard. "NUM National Office, can I help you?"

The voice said "I'd like to send a donation to the strike fund. Who should I make the cheque out to?"

As I gave him the details I tried to suppress the wish that he might have thought of ringing before he'd spent an evening in the pub. Then his tone turned mocking.

"You see, I'm a police officer, and I'm making so much money from overtime payments because of your strike that I thought I'd donate some of my spare cash to the strike fund."

"Go to hell!" Then as now my swearing vocabulary lacked force, range and imagination.

As I chucked the phone, still connected, onto the table to stop him ringing back, I thought of the terrible hardship our members and their families were suffering. Little food, no heat or hot water, so no hot baths – and that bastard was doing Thatcher's dirty work, then laughing at the poverty of the miners' families. I had trouble getting back to sleep after that call.

Occasionally those late-night calls provided a comedy turn. One night a man rang who seemed to be unconnected to the union and our struggle.

"Is that the miners' union? I want you to give me the phone number that will get me through to Margaret Thatcher in Downing Street. I want to talk to her and they're not letting me through. I've got a serious complaint to make – this time she's gone over the top and I'm not going to stand for it. I'm sure you must have a private phone number for her."

At first I thought this was some sort of joke, perhaps a wind-up to while away a boring night in a strike centre, but as he went on I realised he was serious, if confused.

"I'm sorry, but we're the last people who would have a private phone number for Margaret Thatcher."

"But you must have her number – all I'm asking is that you let me have it. I wouldn't tell anyone where I got it from."

"We've no idea what Margaret Thatcher's phone number is, I'm afraid."

As I finally managed to get him off the phone, I suspected he still believed we were hiding that secret phone number from him. Perhaps he also believed that Arthur Scargill and Peter Heathfield would drop in on Thatcher from time to time for a cup of tea and a friendly chat.

Sometimes those disembodied night voices provided a bit of company. One night I had a call from someone who said he was a miner on duty in one of the Yorkshire Area strike centres. Weary, lonely and bored, I had the strange feeling that we were the only human beings in the world who were awake. Once we had dealt with the business of the call, we carried on chatting. He said he was alone in the Miners' Welfare building that hosted his strike centre, while I told him I was by myself on the tenth floor of the National Office building. Finally, running out of conversation, we ended the call. Then I began to worry. What if he wasn't who he claimed to be? Someone had set fire recently to our building because he had a grievance with the Tax Office housed beneath our rented offices. Because of the fire I knew that the Fire Brigade's ladders were not long enough to reach our floors of the building. What if this alleged miner was outside the building now, planning to break in, knowing I was alone? There was only a single glass door between me and anyone outside who might want to harm me as a way of attacking the union. Finally I could stand it no longer. If I rang the number the "miner" had given me, I should be able to check that he was who he claimed to be. As soon as I got through I recognised his voice, announcing that I had reached the strike centre. Relieved, I confessed that I had begun to worry in case he was not really the person he claimed to be. He then admitted to having the same doubts: wondering who I really was, and whether I was part of a plan to attack his strike centre, knowing he was alone. We started to laugh at ourselves for being over-suspicious.

By day the Control Room was less isolated, as two members of the National Executive Committee shared responsibility for its oversight, taking it in turns to sit with staff during weekdays, leaving a sole staff member on duty each evening, night and over weekends. Unlike the rest of the National Executive, John Weaver from Yorkshire and Wes Chambers from Kent were not Area Officials with associated responsibilities and high incomes. As underground workers, Johnny and Wes were in touch with the concerns of our rank and file members. During one boring afternoon Johnny offered to read my palm, a skill he had picked up somewhere.

"Go on then, Johnny, you can tell me my future."

"Now, let's have your hand – it needs to be your left. Let's see..."

As Johnny always exuded good will and an air of kindness, the atmosphere had been jovial, but as he studied my hand his face began to tighten. There was a long silence.

"Well, what can you see?"

I wondered if he was teasing me, but all the same I felt a bit uneasy. He looked at me, his face troubled, and said

"No, I can't tell you."

"Go on, it can't be that bad, can it?"

"No, no, I can't say any more. Let's talk about something else".

He seemed really upset, but refused to say why, so I never found out what he thought he'd seen. As a bit of fun to while away some time on Control Room duty, palm-reading had certainly proved a flop.

The other NEC member overseeing the Control Room was Wes Chambers from Kent. As he was so far from home he had to stay in a Sheffield hotel during the week. Quite properly, the NUM covered his expenses there. One morning, bumping into Wes as I left the office, I explained that I had been on duty for more than twenty- four hours, so I was going home to sleep. He grinned sympathetically, then said

"Never mind, at least you're making money from the overtime pay." I looked at him, startled.

"But we don't get overtime pay, Wes."

"Don't have me on – they must be paying you overtime."

"No staff member gets overtime pay, however much extra time we put in. Arthur Scargill abolished overtime pay for National Office staff when they moved up to Sheffield."

"But they must pay you something for all these extra hours you put in."

"No, Wes, we never get a penny in overtime pay."

I left him looking very thoughtful.

Call for return to work without a settlement   Throughout the year of the strike, it had been terribly damaged by "working miners", whose numbers grew in its later months. These were not being reported accurately, though. By the start of 1985 we knew that the Coal Board had been manipulating their announcements about numbers of miners returning to work for a long time. Their figures were so crooked that George Bolton, a full- time official from Scottish Area remarked caustically: "Every time a pit cat walks across the yard they put it down as another man back to work."

Although we knew the Coal Board figures were wrong, our own Industrial Relations Department was collecting figures showing that more and more of our members were returning to work. Enter stage right Kim Howells, a senior staff member in South Wales Area. In front of TV cameras Kim called repeatedly for the NUM to return to work without a settlement. Our own private counting indicated that his calls were being followed by increasing numbers returning to work. What was Kim Howells up to? As a staff member he had no right to make policy statements to press and TV. Nor was he entitled to take part in any decision-making meetings. If we National Office staff had spoken to the media we would have been dismissed. I heard some NEC members, just before a meeting, challenge South Wales elected officials about Kim's public statements, but General Secretary George Rees just brushed it off.

"Well, he got a bit carried away..." was all George would say.

He knew that Kim could not be challenged personally by NEC members because Kim, not entitled to attend NEC meetings, never appeared in Sheffield. I never believed George Rees was so weak as to allow Kim to get away with such behaviour against the wishes of the Area leadership. I thought that the South Wales elected Area officials in fact supported Kim's repeated statements that our members should return to work without a settlement. It seemed cowardly of them not to admit their real views, but to hide behind a staff member. Where had this idea of a return to work without a settlement come from?

Years later Seumas Milne discovered an important memo from David Hart to both MacGregor and Thatcher. In Autumn 1984 he wrote that it was essential that the NUM be forced to return to work without a settlement.

Milne quotes a claim by Brian Crozier, whom he describes as "the freelance MI6 agent and confidant of Margaret Thatcher, Ronald Reagan and CIA director Bill Casey". Crozier claimed that Hart had "indirect but reliable access to two members of the NUM Executive" throughout the strike. Who were those NEC members, and who was the go-between connecting Hart with them? Whatever the answers to these questions, I had no inkling during the strike that David Hart was the author of "return to work without a settlement". It seemed a peculiar idea to me, as I had thought there was always a settlement, whether that represented success or failure, or something in between, for the union concerned.

How had Kim Howells got hold of that idea? Did he know its origin in David Hart, Thatcher's fixer? Many years after the strike I wrote to Kim Howells, asking if he knew where that idea had originated. My query was neither acknowledged nor answered.

End of the strike and its aftermath The final traumatic Special Delegate Conference of the strike, with its narrow victory for return to work without a settlement, was held on March 3, 1985 at Congress house in London, headquarters of the TUC. The last day of the strike was set for the following day, Monday, to allow time to ensure a unified and dignified return to work on Tuesday. Whole NUM branches and their supporters marched to the pits with banners held high and bands playing. Every time I watched this on the news I shed tears. In some places, though, the return to work was messy. Kent Area sent pickets to Yorkshire on that Tuesday morning. Their view was that to return to work with hundreds of members still dismissed would be treachery, although they had no proposals about how to force the Coal Board to re-employ our sacked members, when a year on strike had failed to bring that about. The Kent picket line called a halt to the march back, led by Arthur Scargill, at one Yorkshire pit, because those miners would not cross a picket line. Even at pits where there was a mass return to work, some individuals could not bring themselves to return because they felt they would be abandoning our sacked members. It took some little time, lots of behind-the-scenes persuasion from union officials, and sometimes threats of dismissal from management, to get everyone back to work. Scotland refused to return to work immediately.

Our members still hold a range of opinions about the strike. Some former strikers look back on that time as the period of their lives when they knew what they were fighting for and felt proud because it was a just cause. Some recall reaching a new understanding about the use of state power. One Derbyshire miner recalls that if you were in desperate need during the strike there was always somewhere you could go to get help. Others find memories of the hardship very painful, while some would prefer not to remember the strike at all. Some of our members, such as those in Notts and Leicestershire, who did not join the strike because they believed their pits would be safe, were to be surprised by the mass closures that followed over the next few years. Some of those had abandoned the NUM for the breakaway UDM.

Miners were returning to work after eighteen months of severe hardship: hunger, shortage of clothes, cold houses, no hot water for baths. By that time many had lost houses, marriages or both. What had they gained in return for such losses? They had two things to celebrate: their sense of having done the right thing, and their knowledge that they had endured longer than anyone would have believed possible. The relatively few strikers in Nottinghamshire, more beleaguered than most, had coined a phrase for their group: Loyal to the Last. It is still used there proudly to describe anyone who stayed solid to the NUM during the strike.

At this point we had hundreds of "sacked lads" who had often been dismissed merely for being in the wrong place at the wrong time. After the return to work NUM Area Officials worked hard for months, with varying levels of success, to get our sacked members re-instated. The Coal Board Area Director in Scotland had vowed that not a single sacked miner there would be reinstated or even re-engaged.

The NEC was instructed by the final Special Delegate Conference of the strike to set up a trust fund to support sacked members and prepare for the future. I was involved in preparing a leaflet urging our members to vote in a ballot for a weekly levy of all members who still had jobs. That money would be used to support our sacked members. Our striker members, with creditors banging on their doors now they had begun to earn once more, seemed to be in no mood to help support our dismissed members. Our members who had worked throughout the strike wanted nothing to do with supporting our sacked lads either. To our great embarrassment and anger we lost that ballot so our dismissed members were left without meaningful financial support from the NUM. Fortunately the Justice for Mineworkers Campaign and other organisations worked for years afterwards to provide assistance, but I felt, along with others, that we as a union had failed our dismissed members.

9 Solidarity efforts and their undermining

Rail unions Sometimes the Control Room played a valuable role in linking us with other unions, in those days before almost everyone had computers and mobile phones. It provided a single point where other unions could be sure of having their queries dealt with quickly. One day Marilyn the telephonist came on the line, saying "I've got Ray Buckton for you, Hilary."

Ray was General Secretary of ASLEF, the train drivers' union. Expecting his PA or secretary, I was surprised to hear Ray's unmistakable northern voice, his accent similar to mine.

"My members are refusing to move some coal until we're sure the NUM has approved it."

This was a delicate issue, as some NUM leaders believed we should stop all movements of coal, even to power stations or steelworks, while others thought we should allow in just enough coal to keep those plants ticking over.

"Management has told our members that the NUM has approved this coal movement, but I've told our members that we move nothing until I've had a personal assurance from your union that it's all right to move it. Is it or isn't it all right?"

Now here was real commitment. Ray was ringing in person to make sure his members were not being misled into undermining our strike. Checking with him the location of the coal, I promised to ring back when I had spoken to one of the National Officials. After hurrying off to consult one, I was able to assure Ray that the coal movement had been sanctioned. Under his determined leadership many ASLEF members withstood tremendous pressures from their employers when they took action to support the mineworkers. In the other rail union, NUR, members were equally firm in refusing to move coal, coke or oil trains without approval from the NUM. They were under enormous pressure in Shirebroook, Derbyshire, which was a flashpoint between striking miners and scabs. Here full-time officials of both rail unions held meetings of both unions together, supplemented by several personal visits from their national leaders Jimmy Knapp and Ray Buckton. British Rail management at Shirebrook tried to intimidate rail union members. They had train crews taken by coach to local power stations to convince them that the large amount of coal being transported by road would never return to rail unless the rail unions abandoned their solidarity action. Despite that blackmail they stood by us.

Shirebrook was not the only place where rail unions held firm. An NUR Branch Secretary told a solidarity conference:

"My members at Coalville have not moved any coal by rail in the Leicestershire coalfield for thirty-two weeks. We're in the middle of a working coalfield, but we've been holding back half the production from Leicestershire. Virtually every pub and club in Coalville has barred us." That referred to the social exclusion faced in the working areas by striking miners and those taking solidarity action in their support. In Leicestershire there were only thirty strikers.

We needed solidarity action by many other unions, too, once our union's funds had been sequestrated, then later put into receivership, or in effect seized by the state. This meant we had no access to our own money. The Official Receiver, a Tory named Michael Arnold, declared "I am the NUM." The Coal Board paid over to Michael Arnold the union dues deducted through the check-off system from the pay of those NUM members who were strikebreaking. Apparently Arnold used those monies to set up an office in London, although we could never work out what was done there. Back in the real NUM National Office in Sheffield, we staff members continued our work as before, but found we were breaking the law by doing just that. Our leaders faced a stark choice: either surrender our struggle or find ways to access the money we needed to keep our work going and provide services to our members.

A new and significant expense was solicitors' fees for the huge number of members who were arrested under Thatcher's Law.

Because of the manipulation of the law to suit the Government's purpose, the banking system was barred to us. Our union needed large amounts of cash just to continue its operations. We staff members were paid in cash handed over in brown envelopes. Knowing that under Thatcher's Law the NUM's only sources of money were illegal, we never asked where this cash came from. During the strike I had learned that the law and morality were radically different, so I never worried about the illegal and unknown sources of my pay. I assumed, accurately, that our leaders had sought help from other unions in our time of desperate need. Because of the brutal and all-encompassing nature of Thatcher's Law, such help would require those other unions to defy court rulings too.

The National Union of Railwaymen (NUR) was one of the unions giving such generous and risky support to us. One day Derbyshire lay official John Walton was asked to travel to London with two other trusted NUM members. Driving Area Secretary Gordon Butler's car to NUR headquarters, they were given £200,000 in cash by General Secretary Jimmy Knapp. This was witnessed by the Executive, presumably because the NUR could not risk making an official written record of such a loan, which of course would have to be repaid later. John understood that half the money was to go to NUM National Office, the remainder to Derbyshire Area NUM. Sometime after that episode, a report appeared in the Financial Times stating that the Government was looking to prosecute those three Derbyshire miners for breaking the terms of the sequestration order. Fortunately that threat was never carried out.

Seafarers Not all solidarity had to be given secretly. Although I was aware that members of several other unions were openly giving us magnificent support, the sheer scale of venomous attacks on the NUM sometimes prevented my understanding and full appreciation of their solidarity efforts. I sensed that my colleagues at National Office were experiencing similar feelings of exhaustion in the toxic atmosphere created by Government, with mass media outlets acting as their complicit megaphones. It was not until the summer of 1985 when Jim Slater, leader of Britain's National Union of Seamen, addressed our Annual Conference that I could begin to appreciate just how much solidarity had been offered by his members. Jim told us that NUS support began in February 1984, following a letter from the NUM asking them not to load coal during our overtime ban. NUS had telexed their members worldwide, instructing them that no coal destined for Britain was to be transported from anywhere in the world. He continued

"On 20th March the first major contingent of coal attempted to move by hundreds of lorries from the Continent on the cross-Channel ferries. Our members immediately turned them back. I remember at the time I went over there were hundreds of lorries spread all over the continental side trying to shift them from Cherbourg and then up to Dunkirk and by all means to get the coal across, and in the end our crews told the ferry companies "unless you decide not to bring in this coal and comply with our support for the miners, then we will stop all passages across to the Continent" and of course that would have included the 60 million passengers a year crossing through the Port of Dover... Needless to say, they immediately conceded to those demands made by our members, and the ferries right throughout the dispute made sure no coal came across in lorries or containers or otherwise.

On 28th March the whole of the North East collier trade had been brought to a standstill. Eighteen large colliers were lying idle in the Tyne, the Tees, the Thames and the Medway. They remained there for one year, until the strike was finished.

During the course of the strike we were dragged through the High Court in London three times. We can testify to the (international) support you received... especially from colleagues in Australia, New Zealand, Denmark and France."

The tremendous reception given by our Conference delegates to Jim's speech showed how much we valued the solidarity of his members. In that summer of 1985 we were all badly in need of a morale-booster. Tragically, the magnificent support from the NUS had not completely prevented the import of coal during the strike. Large quantities had been brought in on tiny boats, crewed by non-union labour. They were then unloaded into dozens of miniscule harbours, lacking unionised registered dockers, where normally only fish was landed. A friend in Devon had told me he could see this happening near his home, while similar reports had come in from other coastal areas. These irregular imports, added to coal supplies coming by road from coalfields such as Nottinghamshire, Leicestershire and South Derbyshire, where most miners were still working, had proved fatal to our struggle.

Print unions We had wonderful moral and practical support from the print unions and other workers on Fleet Street where national newspapers were printed then. As well as sending food aid throughout the strike, Fleet Street print unions mounted a dramatic episode of solidarity action. The Sun, full of bile against the miners, had commissioned or found a photo showing Arthur Scargill with his hand raised, waving to a crowd. The photographer, obviously with malign intent, had snapped it just at the moment when Scargill's open-handed wave looked like a Hitler salute. Intended for a prominent place on the front page, this image was too much for the printers to stomach. As they knew Arthur Scargill would never give a fascist salute they simply refused to print the photograph, defying all sorts of threats from management. Eventually the Sun was published with a blank space where the photo should have been, accompanied by a caption stating that printers had refused to process a photo. Management and owners were clearly livid, so in the staff kitchen at National Office we enjoyed some rare minutes of celebration that day. Knowing that the print workers had only prevented publication of the photo through their tight union organisation, we admired them whilst being very grateful.

There were other ways in which Fleet Street print workers helped us. During the bleak period leading up to Christmas 1984 they raised large sums of money, then bought huge quantities of food and children's toys that were loaded onto a fleet of lorries, each bearing a poster promising "They shall not starve". The lorries were driven up the M1 in convoy to the North Derbyshire Women's Action Group base for distribution so that each family had some Christmas food and toys for their kids. This gift provided both emotional and practical support for our hard-pressed members and their families, although the physical and logistical effort involved in distributing those solidarity gifts was very tiring for Women's Action Group activists. The print unions sent supplies to other Areas including Bassetlaw, where striking miners' families were delighted to receive Christmas presents for their children.

When Shireoaks colliery was organising a march from Bassetlaw to London, branch officer George Bell needed to travel there to make arrangements. He met some London printworkers who managed somehow to get him a press pass from the Telegraph so he could enter the Fleet Street building. They told him he could use the boiler house on the roof as a place to sleep, instead of paying for accommodation. When the marchers reached London, supported all the way by solidarity action, printworkers marched with them as far as County Hall, where they were welcomed by Greater London Council Leader Ken Livingstone. Ken, like David Blunkett of South Yorkshire Council in those days, could always be relied upon to support progressive causes. Perhaps that is why Thatcher's Government later abolished both Local Authorities, which had policies, such as cheap fares, that she regarded as threats to democracy.

Individuals Sometimes valuable solidarity could be given in a low-key way by individuals. John Burrows, a full-time official in Derbyshire, recalls meeting a member of banking union

BIFU. When he explained how many of our members were in desperate situations, about to lose their houses because they could not pay their mortgages, she was able to help. Pointing out that she and her colleagues always had large piles of foreclosure notices on their desks, she said that she and her colleagues would check if the defaulting residents were miners. If they were, their documents would be placed on the bottom of the pile to delay the process. When their documents finally reached the top of the pile, they would be moved back down to the bottom again, so the forced sales of miners' homes would never happen at their branch of the bank.

On a trip to London to arrange a march from Shireoaks to the capital, George Bell met a taxi driver who promised to take his children round the capital's tourist attractions without any charge if George could get them to London. That promise was honoured. Many others made great individual sacrifices to support striking miners. Soon after the start of the strike a pensioner came up to our seventh-floor office and donated £10 to the Solidarity Fund. We all felt touched at such generosity, as £10 was a huge amount for a pensioner to give away at that time. It showed once again that often those who have least will give most. Other individuals made great efforts over a long period. On a rare weekend away with friends in London, I was taken down a street in Harlesden to the pavement in front of Woolworths. There I was introduced to a local hero, an ASLEF member who stood there collecting money for the miners, week after week throughout the strike. Despite being pestered by the police about permits for his collections he never gave up, raising large sums for us. Although I thanked him for his efforts I knew he was acting out of an ingrained sense of solidarity, not because he wanted thanks.

In Chesterfield many trades unionists understood that there were two reasons to assist the miners. One was to offer solidarity, the other was to help preserve their own industries such as engineering, which depended on mining for their continued existence. Rob Rawdon, an engineer at Markhams, which manufactured essential equipment such as winding wheels for local pits, stood in his workplace every week making a bucket collection for the miners. He was disappointed to find some of his workmates failed to see that as mining formed the bedrock of their work it was important to support the miners' attempt to keep pits open. Rob took no comfort from being proved right when the end of mining brought the closure of Markhams. Tony Priest, a Chesterfield resident who was a member of both the Labour Party and white-collar union ASTMS, also worked hard for our members. He would cycle around Boythorpe, a working-class area of the town, collecting weekly donations. Some vicars, such as Rodney Marshall of Goldthorpe in South Yorkshire, gave us valuable support over that whole period. Rod was nicknamed "the red vicar" by his local newspaper. George Bell and three other striking miners from Shireoaks went to support the strikers in Easington, County Durham, where police behaved notoriously badly. They were put up in the home of the local vicar, who loathed the police because of the way they behaved.

As it was part of my job to deal with members of the public who rang our offices in connection with the strike, I took a call one day from a woman living in what southerners call the Home Counties.

"My friend and I were journalists and NUJ members before we were married, so we thought we might offer to help you."

"Well, thanks very much, that's good of you. Our striking members are short of food and clothes. They desperately need baby food and baby clothes, nappies, pushchairs – "

She broke in on my list with

"I'd no idea things were so bad. My husband's *Daily Telegraph* isn't telling us anything like that."

I took a breath, then responded gently

"No, your husband's *Daily Telegraph* won't be telling you anything like that, but it's true all the same. Our members are really suffering."

She sounded shocked and upset, promising that she and her friend would collect money for the Solidarity Fund. Not all callers were as helpful, though. One day I took a call from someone claiming to be a doctor who alleged that some of our pickets had refused to let him pass to reach some patients. I didn't even try to hide my disbelief.

"Why would our members do that? They know better than most people, because of accidents down the pit, how important it is for doctors to reach patients. Our members wouldn't want to get in the way of a doctor."

He kept arguing, I kept openly disbelieving him, never being able to understand who he was and why he was making such a claim.

Women's groups Once the strike began grassroots women's groups started to grow in the coalfields. They set up communal kitchens and prepared food parcels, persuading food shops to offer discounts for their bulk-buying operations. Local shops, whether independents or branches of large chains, had an interest in offering such discounts in strike areas because their takings had plummeted once miners had little or no income. Soon the sheer scale of need, with their children hungry and needing new clothes, forced the women's groups to expand their activities. They began hunting for donations of second-hand clothes, shoes, children's pushchairs and babies' bottles. Thatcher's Law had cut benefits for striking workers to zero, but even Thatcher's Law could not stop babies being born into mining families. Arthur Scargill, Peter Heathfield and many Area Officials began to praise the women's groups, while at the same time many local strike centres were starting to see the value of their work. The activities of the coalfield women's support groups were integral to the strike effort.

Sometimes those support groups were created initially by men as well as women. In Mansfield, the centre of the Nottinghamshire coalfield, the support group founders were two women, Ida Hackett and Julie Wilkinson, and two men, Ernie Daglish and Andy Miller. Both Ida and Ernie were members of the Communist Party. Their aim was to involve men and women from the mining area, but over time the group became more and more a women's organisation, so Ernie and Andy withdrew to leave space on the committee for women. Their central group co-ordinated the work of the thirty colliery-based Nottinghamshire women's support groups, covering every mining community in that coalfield. They were quickly given office space by the public-service workers' union NUPE at their office near Nottingham city centre. Telephones, photocopying and other facilities were also made available free of charge, which was a very generous commitment by NUPE. The central women's group seemed to attract extra help from women living in the city, with regular Saturday morning fund-raising stalls held next to St Peter's Church. On at least one occasion, when some people were causing trouble at the stall, the women were helped by others on the nearby CND stall.

There were other women in mining families who made essential contributions to the strike: the women who went out to work in jobs outside the industry, bringing in wages to keep their families fed and clothed. Those women became sole family breadwinners for that long year. For instance Maureen Eaton, married to one of the Nottinghamshire Loyal to the Last strikers at Newstead Colliery, got herself a factory job once Eric's wage had vanished. Christina Bell, already a home support worker for the County Council, became sole family breadwinner when her husband George was on strike for the full year at Shireoaks Colliery in Bassetlaw. Many more women were in this position. Their heroic contribution to the endurance test of the strike was just as valuable as that of women in the Women's Support Groups, although it has usually passed unnoticed by outsiders or historians.

Quite often men and women worked together to bulk-buy and transport food for the kitchens or to give out food parcels. Such joint work often led to a new acceptance of women as equal partners in the strike. For instance, in autumn 1984 a weekend conference of activists was organised in Durham, with men and women from both Durham and South Wales participating. Kim Howells of South Wales told the meeting that food parcel distribution in his patch involved men as well as women. They were using those activities as opportunities to discuss the reasons for the strike and the need to keep it going, as not every striking member was actively involved and well-informed. Kim pointed out that it was the women in South Wales who were leading that use of discussion alongside food distribution. Such an acceptance of women as valued partners in the strike was regrettably not universal. A Yorkshire strike committee meeting clearly disapproved of women picketing, as they decided that women arrested on the picket line would only receive legal support from NUM solicitors if they had been authorised to picket by the union. The implication was that women who were not even NUM members should ask permission from the NUM before they mounted or joined a picket line. That decision caused such anger that it was later overturned.

Some of the women in grassroots coalfield support groups had previously been involved in politics or campaigns. In Chesterfield the Women's Action Group grew out of the Women's Canvass Team that helped Tony Benn's election as MP for Chesterfield early in 1984. Although I had been part of that team, once the strike began I was spending too many hours at National Office in Sheffield to be able to play a part in Chesterfield Women's Action Group. In Notts the leaders of the grassroots women's support groups, such as Ida Hackett and Liz Hollis, were already seasoned campaigners. Some women, though, were new to that type of activity, so worked very hard as they developed new skills. Debbie Coulter, a striking miner's wife from South Yorkshire, was nervous about making her first-ever speech at a rally. I suggested she should win sympathy from the audience by admitting it was the first time she had spoken in public. She took that advice, was doing brilliantly, then suddenly said calmly "I'm going to stop now, because I can't carry on any longer." There was lots of applause as she walked steadily off the stage, but I felt a bit concerned, especially when I saw her sitting on the floor in the wings, looking unwell.

"You were great, Debbie, but are you alright?"

She looked up.

"I felt really nervous before I started, so I had a cigarette."

I waited, not quite understanding her problem.

"But I don't smoke, so it made me feel sick. I didn't want to risk being ill in front of everybody…"

I really felt for her, reminding her how well she had done to keep calm and in control of the situation. After that excellent start Debbie continued to develop her confidence and skills, in time becoming a full-time officer of the GMB union.

In County Durham Heather Wood, chairperson of the local Constituency Labour Party, worked with others in 1983 to create the magnificent community group Save Easington Area Mines (SEAM). Once the strike started those activists realised the crucial importance of women as part of the strike effort, so they wrote to every woman in the area, urging their involvement. Women's support groups then developed around each colliery in the area. Invited up to Easington to speak to one of the large SEAM public meetings, I had felt nervous about giving a speech. but was impressed by the large attendance and enthusiasm of the audience. SEAM clearly involved men as well as women. When I told them about the donation of £10 by a pensioner, I saw a woman in the front row shedding tears. The realisation that I could reach an audience on an emotional level boosted my confidence, so I never again felt so nervous about making a speech. Many miners' families generously acted as hosts to travelling speakers, so after that SEAM meeting I was given a bed for the night with the family of NUM member and local councillor Alan Cummings. Relief that my talk had gone well made me sleep so heavily I could not remember where I was when I first woke up the following morning. Alan's wife gave me breakfast and seemed quite happy to agree when I asked tentatively if it would be alright to have a bath. Once they were on strike, miners were not allowed their usual concessionary coal, so their families were short of heat and hot water. Kowing this, I silently hoped a bath would not be my extravagance at their expense. Labour leader of Easington Council John Cummings, with his little dog, collected me for a visit to a friendly, jovial picket line before I caught the train home. A former miner, John was well-known to the pickets and clearly worked hard to support the strike.

There were other women's support groups, such as the Sheffield group, whose members sometimes came from outside the coal industry. At that time Government's Manpower Services Commission had been moved to the city, where there was a left-wing council. Sheffield became popular for a time in leftish circles, so several Sheffield Women's Support Group members, experienced in the women's movement, had come to the city from London. One participant, active locally in the labour movement as well as in the Shefield Women's Support Group, recalls that she sometimes felt over-awed by the confidence of those middle-class women. Some had been experienced and dedicated activists at Greenham Common. Relationships between the different kinds of women were generally positive and they used their magnificent organising skills to support the strike and each other. Members of Sheffield Women Against Pit Closures were not only offering moral and political support, but also gave practical help to the NUM by fundraising as well as preparing and serving refreshments for our members attending gatherings at City Hall. They used the Sheffield Centre Against Unemployment (SCAU) building, almost next door, for those activities. SCAU always actively supported labour movement campaigns.

The first national mining women's demonstration was held on May 12 in Barnsley. Its advertising leaflet proudly announced "Women to lead the demonstration". I loved marching down the street that day, partly because it was the women's march, partly because I had no responsibility for organising it, so I was free to just enjoy the moment. We ended with an indoor rally in the Barnsley Civic Hall, in a spirit so buoyant it felt as if the roof would lift off.

On the weekend of November 10 and 11 the various Women's Support Groups held a national meeting in Chesterfield Queen's Park Cricket Pavilion, with the assistance of Council Leader Bill Flanagan, who gave permission for its use. Bill never missed an opportunity to help us. Delegates were to sleep there overnight. I could not resist walking across the park to see what was happening. Police officers from other parts of the country, imported to keep the miners down, were billeted just yards away, across the road in the Territorial Army Drill Hall, so I was concerned when I saw men hanging about near the cricket pavilion. Who were they and what were they up to? When I asked one of them what was happening he told me they were miners who would be staying outside the pavilion all night to make sure the women were safe. That was a great relief, although I felt for those guardian miners who would have an uncomfortable night, standing in the cold on an unusual type of picket duty. Later the national grouping of women's organisations named itself Women against Pit Closures (WAPC). Kate Alvey of Chesterfield recalls that they voted against the WAPC name because they thought it too restrictive. Its stated aims included developing the organisation of working-class women and campaigning on issues affecting their communities, including peace, public services, solidarity with the unemployed and Black people.

North Derbyshire Women's Action Group (WAG), a co-ordinating organisation of women's support groups from every pit village in North Derbyshire, was based initially in the Chesterfield Labour Club, just across the road from North Derbyshire NUM Offices. At the start of the strike its members provided a daily soup run for pickets in the surrounding area, but as time went on their activities expanded dramatically in response to growing need. They negotiated lower prices for bulk-buying so they could provide weekly food parcels. As more and more miners were given bail conditions that forbade picketing, WAG began to join and organise pickets. Their operation quickly outgrew the Labour Club, so Council leader Bill Flanagan, ever supportive, gave permission for them to use the Borough Council's Goldwell Rooms just along the road from the Club and the Miners' offices.

The labour movement in localities   For many years Chesterfield had prided itself on organising the biggest and best May Day celebrations in the country, but in 1984 Trades Council excelled itself, with 10,000 on the march to show solidarity with our strike. Much later in the year when strikers were suffering great hardship Trades Council invited a Women's Action Group representative to speak. As usual, Trades Council was meeting in the Council Chamber of the Miners' Offices, where Kate Alvey, a miner's wife and WAG activist, brought along us one of their weekly food parcels. It was a plastic supermarket bag containing the pitifully small amount of food that was all the women could afford to supply to each striker. She explained their urgent need for more money. My partner Barry Johnson, Trades Council President, picked up the bag, waving it in the air as he declared

"This is our shame. We must raise more money for the miners, or they'll be starved back to work."

I added my pleas to those of Barry. We both knew the importance of this battle for the future of the entire labour movement, not only for the miners themselves. The discussion that followed showed some delegates were unwilling to support the miners, while one delegate accused us of haranguing the meeting. My feeling was that our accuser knew he was in the wrong but was unwilling to face up to his failure of solidarity. Neither Barry nor I felt guilty about urging Trades Council to give more help to the striking miners so they and their families could have more to eat.

Some people within Chesterfield's labour movement gave magnificent support to miners and their families. Huge numbers of our members were being arrested on picket lines, often for little or no reason. One night in Chesterfield Labour Club, the wife of a miner who had been hauled up in court was very upset, feeling shamed by her husband's appearance in the dock. Someone in our group knew just how to make her feel better. He was veteran trade union leader Baz Barker, revered because he had done so much to build the engineering union in our town. Baz explained that she had no need to feel ashamed, as her husband was quite right to be fighting for his job and for a future where their kids would have jobs too. Although her husband had done nothing wrong, the police and the courts would always act to support the employers and try to punish strikers. That seemed to comfort her.

Other labour movement figures had powers to offer practical, as well as moral, support. As Christmas approached, Chesterfield's Council Leader Bill Flanagan had discovered that the Borough was empowered to spend money to relieve hardship. He then instructed officers to find funds that would achieve that end, so £50,000 was given by the Council to assist families in the mining community who lived within the Borough. This helped many desperate strikers through the Christmas period. Similar help was provided over that period in Strathclyde, where the Regional Council gave £10,000 to relieve miners' hardship. Local councillors paid personally for miners' children to attend the Mother Goose pantomime in Ayr. In North Notts, Bassetlaw District Council gave the NUM an office, where Shireoaks striking miner Glyn Gilfoyle was installed as advice worker to help strikers wring out of the Government every penny of the miserly benefits allowed by the law.

The steel city of Sheffield also distinguished itself by its support for our striking members. Once Arthur Scargill had re-located National Office away from London, with most of its staff having chosen not to move north, we had many new staff members, including myself, who lived in or around Sheffield. As in Chesterfield, the Trades Council was strong but because the city was much bigger, more resources could be mustered to help us. Sheffield Trades Council was at that time a powerful body because the steel and cutlery industries were large and well-organised. In those days there would have been no need to explain the meaning of the term "well-organised". It meant that most, often all, workers were members of appropriate trade unions, recognised by employers, which were active and able to defend their members' terms and conditions of employment. Trades Councils were representative bodies that co-ordinated discussion and action between all the TUC-affiliated unions within a locality, as well as easing liaison between TUC headquarters at Congress House and its local affiliated unions. Although many of the workers in Sheffield's heavy industries were men, their elected Trades Council President was a woman. That alone was a tribute to her standing in the trade union movement, as well as to her abilities and commitment. Although I did not know Blanche Flannery personally, I always heard her spoken of with great respect, while under her leadership Sheffield Trades Council was a vital and energetic part of the TUC's Yorkshire and Humberside Region.

Giving a welcome address to our 1985 National Conference, which for reasons of economy was held in Sheffield, Blanche was thanked by our President for her work. Arthur Scargill pointed out that she had supported the NUM over many years, as well as joining our members on picket lines. Banche told us that as the strike began Trades Council had set up a broad committee of local unions, women's support groups in the pit villages, Sheffield Women Against Pit Closures (SWAPC), Yorkshire Area NUM Executive and the City Council. This body met weekly throughout the strike and for several weeks afterwards. Although I had been aware of Sheffield Trades Council's support for us, I had not realised how many other partners they had drawn in to help us, nor how closely they had worked with Yorkshire NUM Area. Blanche told our Conference that they had raised many thousands of pounds for our striking members. Trades Council also arranged direct contacts between factories, strikers' food kitchens and pit villages, as well as issuing many leaflets to Sheffield's residents. Overseen by Blanche as part of the Trades Council solidarity effort, Percy Riley led a team who staffed a solidarity stall on Fargate. They worked through heat, rain and snow, giving out leaflets, engaging in friendly chat with passers-by, becoming a fixture of city centre life as they raised large sums of money to relieve the hardship being felt by our strikers. Most days I would stop and talk to them, grateful for their sustained commitment. Although I had no idea Percy had been forced by ill-health to retire from the Coal Board's Fence workshops before the start of the strike, I began to worry about his health when I found him one day sitting on our cold marble office staircase with an ashen face.

"Percy, what's the matter? Are you ill? Can I get you anything?"

"I just needed a rest, I'll be all right in a minute or two."

Although he made light of his pain, Percy was in fact becoming very ill, dying early in 1986 after a lifetime of service to the labour movement.

As Blanche spoke to our Conference in the summer of 1985, she pointed out that they were continuing to support our many victimised members, which was heartening and impressive. It seems, though, that Blanche was being over-modest, because only recently her daughter Kate, who had herself been very active in Sheffield Women Against Pit Closures and in solidarity work in the trade union movement, recalled many more of her mother's achievements as Trades Council President. In July 1984 a convoy of twenty-four buses, led by SWAPC, took people bearing £1000-worth of goods to twelve different strike centres in the Notts coalfield. Those empty buses then carried strikers and their families to a gala on the Nottingham Goose fair site. The buses were sponsored by shop stewards at some of Sheffield's largest workplaces: Shardlows, Firth Derihon, Firth Brown and Forgemasters, while the city's NALGO Local Government branch, NUPE and Centre Against Unemployment also provided support. Given Neil Kinnock's distaste for the strike, he would not have been pleased to hear that Heeley and Sheffield Central Constituency Labour Parties had also been involved in that massive show of solidarity. Later a gathering at Sheffield City Hall built a food mountain that was delivered to various pits. Because the City Council, led by David Blunkett, had been involved in the solidarity committee from the start they knew that 1500 miners living in the city were experiencing great hardship, so they distributed £100,000-worth of food vouchers to assist them. Blanche also picketed at Orgreave and worked to build attendance for mass pickets there. Today Kate continues the family tradition of support for the NUM through her work as Secretary of the Orgreave Truth and Justice Campaign.

The third member of the family, Sheffield MP Martin Flannery, also working extremely hard to support us, was much in demand as a speaker and a presence at events. Other Sheffield MPs Bill Michie and Richard Caborn also provided vital help. Along with David Blunkett, they were trustees of the Miners' Solidarity Fund, which had to be set up as an entity separate from our union to prevent the state from taking money donated to relieve the terrible poverty of our strikers. The courts, operating under Thatcher's Law, had taken our main NUM funds into their iron grip. With Danny O'Connor, our Head of Social Insurance, I was involved with the Solidarity Fund Trustees. As David Blunkett was fully occupied in leading Sheffield City Council, we would ask Bill and Richard to meet us, then Danny would tell them how much money was needed in each NUM Area. Trusting in his knowledge and judgement, they would sign cheques for those amounts.

Many other Labour MPs also gave us tremendous support. Dennis Skinner, MP for Bolsover and Tony Benn, our Chesterfield MP, both toured the country speaking, to the point of near-exhaustion. Both their Constituency Labour Parties were strong supporters of the strike. Dennis, always aware of what was happening around his own locality, spoke informally at a North Derbyshire miners' gala in the summer of 1984, giving the highest praise to work done by the local women's support groups. Tony was a regular visitor to both the strike centre and Women's Action Group base, often discussing with Betty Heathfield the various problems encountered by strikers and their families. For instance, one miner's wife said that her husband was wrongly recorded by the Coal Board as still being at work, so Government social security staff were refusing to pay her any benefits for herself and her family. Their excuse was that her husband was allegedly receiving a wage. That had been going on for ten weeks. It is hard to imagine that this "mistake" by colliery management was accidental, particularly when claiming a striking miner as being at work would boost their alleged number of "working miners". Those numbers became part of the Coal Board and Government's propaganda war to pressure even more miners into returning.

On Tyneside the grassroots labour movement also worked hard to provide practical solidarity. Kevin Flynn, a shop steward at Swan Hunters shipyard who also volunteered at the Centre Against Unemployment, remembers their sustained solidarity work. They wanted to make weekly collections in the Newcastle Monument area, favoured by the labour movement as a campaigning space. As it was impossible to obtain permits every week for collections there, public meetings were held instead every week, enabling collections without the need for a permit. With the help of its progressive vicar, daily collections were held on nearby church premises, where police could not interfere.

Despite opposition from sections of their national leaderships, regional and local Labour and Communist Party organisations gave magnificent support to the miners by organising or assisting many of the miners' support groups that sprang up across England, Scotland and Wales. West Derbyshire Labour Party twinned itself with Arkwright Colliery, near

Chesterfield, with some party members regularly joining the picket line at Arkwright, while one joined Policewatch. That was a network of trained volunteer observers, often academics or lawyers, who kept an eye on police behaviour, reporting any breaches of the law by police officers. Policewatch volunteers must have found themselves very busy in that task. Walkley Labour Party in Sheffield held weekly whip-rounds to raise money for the strikers, while at least one member regularly joined the picket line, taking his very small son along too. This level of commitment was also shown right across the country, with London's Brent Trades Council, supported by both local Labour Party and local authority, raising £40,000 for Kent miners over the summer of 1984. An ASLEF member raised £1000 in one day from fellow-workers at Willesden Junction, while the Communist Party in London collected £200 in cash and created a food mountain worth £1500 for Kent miners at an event in Conway Hall and Red Lion Square that summer.

Political Parties Tony Benn's published *Diaries* record his anger at the refusal by Labour Party Leader Neil Kinnock to speak on a single NUM platform during the strike. The one public meeting where Kinnock shared a platform with Scargill seemed to have been organised by the Labour Party in Stoke on Trent.

The opposition of the Labour Party leadership was shown by internal discussions. Some Campaign Group MPs had raised with Kinnock the possibility of a joint NUM and Labour Party campaign about the strike. Kinnock had said this was a matter for the NEC, which agreed a form of words at the end of October. In that short period at least one meeting was held between some of the left-wing Campaign Group of Labour MPs and the three NUM National Officials. As Tony Benn continued to complain about his party leadership's lack of commitment, it seems that party leaders ensured no meaningful action was undertaken by the party as a whole. I was never personally aware of any improvement in the attitude of Labour leadership. There was, though, no doubting the commitment of the Campaign Group of Labour MPs. Another Parliamentary Labour Party figure, Shadow Energy spokesperson Stan Orme, gave us valuable support. He pointed out that a review by five leading accountants showed the Coal Board's accounts to be a mine of misinformation. Collieries described by the Board as uneconomic did not in reality lose money. Any reasonable citizen might have expected such information to be headline news in mainstream media, but somehow that never happened.

As the strike went on elements in the national leadership of the Communist Party of Great Britain seemed, for reasons I never understood, to become more and more critical of the NUM leadership. Just as the strike began Peter Heathfield, newly-elected to the General Secretary post, had taken office, meaning all three National Officials were left-wingers, with NUM Vice-president Mick McGahey a leading member of the CPGB. I expected support, then, for the NUM from the national leadership of my own party. We in the East Midlands Communist Party worked tremendously hard to support the strike, fully involving our miner members, but found ourselves increasingly at odds with our national party leadership. Such CPGB national leadership criticism of the NUM leadership must have caused great stress for Mick McGahey, who was committed to both. That stress sometimes seemed to show itself in his behaviour.

North Derbyshire women's march Once Christmas was over, with increasing numbers of North Derbyshire miners strikebreaking, the Women's Action Group decided that dramatic action was required. They mounted an event called Strike, Alive in 85. Despite arctic weather they marched, day after day, to every pit in the North Derbyshire Area, hoping to encourage the strikers and swell their numbers. Striking miner's wife Sue Walton joined in when she could, wheeling her small son in his pushchair. When John Burrows, the hard-working full-time Derbyshire NUM official, made a general offer of lifts in his car, Sue felt that it would be

disloyal to the other women to climb into a car, so she carried on walking. Yet afterwards, when she realised how cold her little son had become, she felt guilty for not having accepted a lift. After that she managed to find someone else to look after her son, rather than taking him on the march again. Each day the women were joined on the road by Bill Flanagan, while Barry Johnson joined in whenever he could slip away from Chesterfield College for a couple of hours. Both had the utmost respect for the courage of the women in braving the appalling weather to complete their march.

Grassroots links Up and down the coalfields links with other workers and communities were sometimes made at grassroots level, using personal contacts. Bottom Pit in Hucknall received a lot of support from Gill Ellis, a Hucknall-born woman from a mining family. She had moved to the London borough of Newham, so set up a miners' support group there. Money was raised in London, then brought up to Hucknall. When I attended the social evening in the Miners' Welfare, organised to welcome support group members, I could feel the warmth of their reception. Hucknall and Linby, its neighbouring pit, were also supported by donations of £53,500 from the Harlow Miners' Support Group. Just imagine the hard work required to raise that amount of solidarity money.

Solidarity from Black and ethnic minority groups Many Black and Asian groups also offered us heart-warming, stomach-filling solidarity. In the Leicestershire coalfield there were only thirty strikers. Labelled by some "working miner" wit as the Dirty Thirty, the brave little band adopted that name as a badge of pride. Leicester branch of the Indian Workers' Association had invited the Dirty Thirty to send someone to speak to their meeting but the strikers, unsure how to pitch such a speech there, had asked me to speak for them instead. I knew from previous experience at Derby IWA meetings that the hall would be full of people, with children running about, speeches in a language I could not even name, with frequent mention of a word that clearly meant "capitalism". IWA meetings were always highly political. All this would be interspersed with musical interludes. I prepared a short speech that hopefully would fit into such an event. With many of the Dirty Thirty crowded onto the stage next to me, I explained the need to save jobs, describing police and government attacks on us. The audience, experienced in racist behaviour meted out by police, government and employers, understood immediately that we were being given a taste of the medicine which had been forced down their throats over many years. They responded very warmly, with a good collection and a spell of socialising, ending in a lovely surprise. After hearing my speech, one IWA woman member had gone home, collected £200 from her house, then brought it back as a donation to our funds. We felt overwhelmed by such generosity.

Those meetings of different communities, building new understandings and friendships, were happening across Britain. Many miners were for the first time experiencing the appalling brutality, violence and contempt meted out to them by the police. They were starting to understand this was exactly what Black people had been living with for decades. Some NUM branch officials seemed to believe that the Coal Board ensured most pits were all-white environments, with the relatively few ethnic minority miners concentrated in a very small number of pits. Gedling, near Nottingham, known as the pit of many nationalities, was one of those exceptions. During the 1970's faceworker Dave Hewitt had been put into a team whose other members were Black. Remembering that group of men with great warmth, he recalls that the experience changed his whole view of the world. Before then he had never had the opportunity to meet Black people. Bentley, near Doncaster, was another of the apparently small number of pits where Black miners worked.

Nottingham Miners' Support Group   This was separate from the group of women in the city who collected around the Nottinghamshire Women's Support Group. Although it was started by International Marxist Group (IMG) members Jean Holman, Leo Keeley and Richard Skyers, the only founder member who has survived to remember it now is Richard. Group members organised bucket collections at weekends in Hyson Green, a multi-cultural area of the city, where they received a good response. Later they joined pickets outside Ratcliffe-on-Soar power station in the Trent Valley. Richard recalls members of some left-wing groups trying to use the Nottingham Miners' Support Group as a way of recruiting new members, although its founders disapproved of that tactic. Richard, Jean and Carol Keeley tried to build support for striking miners in the National Union of Teachers, but found many of their fellow-teachers, living in relative job security and comfort, failed to see the relevance of the NUM struggle to their own situation. Perhaps today many teachers, having recently experienced their own trade union battles against the government, might react more positively.

Jean and Richard hosted three Yorkshire miners who needed to stay in the city because it was impossible to get past police roadblocks in daily journeys south. Those miners seemed to be picketing Babbington or Cinderhill pits, both within the city boundaries. As well as providing board and lodging, Richard and Jean supplied pocket money to their guests. Although Richard does not say so himself, I can only view this as a very generous commitment to the miners' struggle. One day Jean, a white woman living with Richard who was Black, sat their guests down and explained to them that the black community as a whole was highly committed to supporting the miners. She pointed out that some of their guests' language was racist. After a discussion the Yorkshire miners understood her point and promised that when they returned home they would challenge and tackle racism.

Michael Boyle, involved with the Nottingham Miners' Support Group as part of his work for the local Unemployed Workers' Centre, recalls the Support Group as very diverse, with unemployed activists, Trades Council members, some Labour Party members and peace group members all involved. As he helped arrange accommodation at the Centre for pickets from other coalfields, Michael had opportunities to hear from various coalfields. His discussions with those groups led him to believe that the approaches of the Yorkshire and Kent pickets were different. He saw the Yorkshire miners as relying on the need for loyalty to the NUM, while the Kent miners had more sophisticated, class-based views of the need for unity in the strike. During that period I was invited to speak at a Sunday dinnertime meeting held in one of the Welfares in Kent. Retired Kent General Secretary Jack Dunn and his wife kindly invited me to a meal at their house before I climbed back onto the train. Jack explained that for a long time the Kent leadership had been using travel time on buses, meal breaks or time in the canteen as "time for the union", when activists engaged in chats with other miners about union issues. Perhaps Michael Boyle's observations indicated the success of such an approach.

Solidarity efforts blocked in Nottinghamshire Strikers at some Nottinghamshire and Leicestershire pits were barred from Welfare premises if "working miners" controlled the committees after the start of the strike. Such exclusions could go beyond facilities intended only for miners and their families. At the start of May 1984 Ann Evans, secretary of the Harworth Miners' Action Group in North Notts, complained to MP Joe Ashton and the local Labour Party about the refusal of the Parish Council to allow them to cook meals for hungry striking miners' children in the Parish Hall. She told the local newspaper

"They locked us out of the meeting and would not even tell us the result in person. I got a telephone call to say our request had been turned down." The claim by Harworth Parish Council that it was empowered to exclude Miners' Action Group members from Parish Council meetings because proceedings were "confidential" was totally false. All elected councils must operate in public, with few exceptions to that rule. Harworth Action Group chairperson Christine Brown blamed the presence of three working miners on the Parish Council for the decision.

"The Government are trying to starve us out and this decision amounts to the same thing. ...We know we are in the minority in Harworth and our group is getting little help from within the village. All we want to do is help people who are desperate without food or money."

The Miners' Action Group then applied to Harworth Miners' Welfare Committee for permission to cook and serve food in the Welfare kitchen. They nursed few hopes about the response because two "working miner" members of the Parish Council also sat on the Welfare committee alongside the colliery manager.

It was not only food kitchens for strikers and their children that were hard to find, though. Michael Boyle, involved in the Nottingham Miners' Support Group, recalls that it was impossible for many strike centres to operate within villages close to their own pits in Nottinghamshire because there was so much hostility from many branch leaderships and committee of the Miners' Welfares. He remembers the Nottingham AEUW office as being the headquarters for South Notts striking miners, while Chesterfield NUM Offices provided the base for North Notts strikers. I can also recall attending Saturday morning meetings of what was termed the Notts Miners' Forum at Chesterfield NUM Offices.

Road haulage Road haulage created another huge hole in the net of solidarity we needed so badly. Many lorry drivers had been enticed into a sort of fake self-employment, with huge loans to pay off on lorries they were buying. In those circumstances they could not afford to turn down any offer of work, even if that meant driving through picket lines. One of our members was killed by a lorry driven recklessly past a picket line. So far as I know, the driver was never prosecuted. One of the points set out in the Ridley Plan had been to insert non-union drivers into the road haulage industry, so perhaps that false self-employment had been a way of carrying out part of the Ridley Plan, although I could never understand quite how it had been achieved. It seemed that by 1984 the T&G were not organising in the small haulage firms that transported large quantities of coal between pits and power stations. The absolute refusal of seafarers and railway workers to shift coal magnified the importance of road haulage, so we could all see that large amounts of scab coal were being taken by road to feed the power stations. Many power stations were located in the Trent valley, close to the Nottinghamshire, South Derbyshire and Leicestershire coalfields, where most of our members were defying the strike call. Although our industrial relations staff noted down the numbers of the strike-breaking lorries in ever-growing piles of ring binders, we were powerless to stop them. Coupled with Government-enabled conversion of some power stations to burn oil as well as coal, our impotence over road transport was another incapacitating blow to our attempts at saving the coal industry, its jobs and communities.

TUC Our National Officials were extremely wary of giving the TUC any power over the conduct of our strike because the TUC had betrayed the miners in 1926. A General Strike that had been called to support the miners, who were then battling pay cuts and a longer working day, had severely disrupted both normal life and the economy. However, the TUC leadership had ended the 1926 General Strike abruptly after nine days without consultation with the miners' union leadership, leaving the miners to be starved back to work after many months of suffering. Yes, miners' memories were long – but rightly so. In 1984-5 our NUM national leaders, then, were trying to balance the need for solidarity from the TUC and its member unions against the danger of granting the TUC that power to betray us once more. We were all aware that because of the number of miners crossing picket lines, it was harder to win support from unions whose leaders were looking for an excuse to take no solidarity action.

Arthur Scargill spoke brilliantly at TUC Congress in September 1984, winning a resolution of support for the NUM, but TUC leadership never transformed that well-intentioned theoretical support into meaningful action. Addressing our NUM Annual Conference in 1985, TUC General Council member Bill Keys, always a good friend to us, pointed out that there had been plenty of emotional support for the miners from other unions, who had raised a great deal of money. His own union SOGAT had raised over a million pounds. Bill correctly pointed out that what had been required was to translate the great flood of feeling into positive industrial action. Although some TUC regions, such as South East and Yorkshire and Humberside, had done their best to assist by organising days of action to support us, tragically that could be no substitute for the sustained solidarity action we needed right across the trade union movement.

Central Electricity Generating Board Despite the magnificent solidarity offered by so many, there were more powerful forces determined to undermine the strike. The CEGB was headed by Lord Marshall who, as the former person in charge of the UK Atomic Energy Authority, was no friend of the coal industry. Under his leadership the nation's power supplies were maintained despite the strike, although it was a close-run contest at times. Thatcher also stuffed her advisory unit with other pro-nuclear power individuals, as well as with pro-oil people, so Marshall was hardly a lone voice. One of our NUM leaflets, issued during the strike in the hope of winning solidarity action from other unions, pointed out that in 1979 a leaked Cabinet Minute had stated "A nuclear programme would have the advantage of removing a substantial proportion of electricity from disruption by miners and the transport workers." Long after the strike I watched in amazement as Lord Marshall admitted in a TV documentary that nuclear power stations had been operated beyond normal maintenance shut-down dates, so risking the catastrophic consequences of a nuclear accident. No trick was too dangerous or dirty for the state to employ in defeating the miners, who were smeared by Thatcher, following the Falklands War victory, as "the enemy within".

The Coal Board's losses would have been wiped out had the price of coal increased by as much as the price of electricity. We pointed this out in a leaflet aimed at other trade union members, but the unfairness in coal and electricity pricing went unheard in the raucous clamour of attacks on striking miners by Government and mainstream media. Despite that constant vilification, surveys conducted during the strike indicated that public support for us was running at between 30% and 40%. Unfortunately, our supporters tended to be trades unionists and other members of the labour movement, so they lacked power in our society.

Electricity industry unions   We desperately needed the support of workers in the electricity-generating power stations. If they had taken solidarity action, power cuts would have immediately followed and we would have been on the way to victory. I had always understood that power station workers were members of the EETPU, led initially by Frank Chapple. Given their leaders' ultra-right political stance, together with their fondness for no-strike agreements with employers, winning EETPU members' support for our industrial action would not be easy, but it was vital. National Office staff produced a draft leaflet aimed at those workers, then submitted it to Nell Myers, Arthur's PA. Eight weeks later it had still not been approved. When Dave Feickert, and Mick Clapham discussed this anxiously in my hearing, they were unsure whether it was Nell or Arthur who was holding up the required approval. Every week that the power stations kept operating normally was more and more damaging to us. Eventually the leaflet was approved, but we feared that by then it was too late. At TUC Congress in September 1984 the new EETPU leader Eric Hammond went on the offensive by attacking the strike and NUM leaders, saying the miners were "lions led by donkeys". Not even an original insult, it still infuriated our delegation, our striking members and the left in general. I assumed that was his intention. Power station workers took no large-scale action to support us, despite NUM leafletting and picketing. It was not until late February 1985 that a grassroots Yorkshire NUM leaflet reported the circulation of a leaflet in Trent Valley power stations "asking the workers to black Yorkshire coal". The leaflet was apparently signed by "Yorkshire Power Station Shop Stewards' Committee and South Yorkshire NUM". This indicates that at least some power station shop stewards were trying to support us despite their national leadership's betrayal of basic trade union solidarity.

Only recently have I learned that some power station workers were in the Transport and General Workers' Union (T&G) rather than EETPU. Bill Hodge, who had been T&G convenor at West Thurrock power station during our strike, spoke recently in public about their "well-organised and political trade union cadre" there. He explained that they thwarted CEGB plans to break the miners' strike by burning oil rather than coal. Despite management pressure and intimidation they held the line, reducing output finally to zero. CEGB was unwilling to take disciplinary action against those trade union members in case that escalated into joint industrial action by power workers and miners. Bill correctly pointed out that if similar action had been taken by workers at two or three other Thames-side power stations, our dispute would have been won because power supplies would have failed. So many years later I have no idea whether Research and Industrial Relations colleagues at National Office were aware that appeals to T&G might have been successful when we were failing to move EETPU members.

NACODS   In autumn 1984 action from a single union, NACODS, could have guaranteed our victory. They organised colliery overmen, deputies and shotfirers. By law, deputies had to be on duty while work was proceeding underground because part of their responsibility was underground safety. Relationships between the NUM and NACODS, as well as between management and unions, varied from Area to Area, pit to pit. At Shireoaks in South Yorkshire Area, where the NUM strike was solid until the time of Labour Party conference in October 1984, relationships between NUM and NACODS were very good. NUM branch official George Bell recalls that NACODS members there would not cross picket lines, even if the picket consisted of a single person. Indeed George would sometimes receive calls from NACODS suggesting that a picket was needed so their members could refuse to cross it while still being paid. Regrettably the situation was very different at neighbouring pit Manton, where the NACODS leader, who had never wanted to stop going underground, seemed determined to resume work as soon as possible. He was unmoved when NUM members tried to persuade him otherwise.

At Abertillery in South Wales, an Area where the strike was solid through most of the strike, there was a good relationship between NUM and NACODS. In that situation, where only a token NUM picket line was needed, the colliery's youngest-ever overman Selwyn Lloyd, along with all the other NACODS men, refused to cross it. He recalls that the pit manager would allow them to go home without loss of pay after those refusals. Once NUM members at Abertillery discovered the NACODS members were being paid, they said it made sense for NACODS to go to work, so stopped asking them not to cross picket lines. NACODS members going underground at that pit posed no threat to the NUM strike because, as no NUM members were willing to break the strike, no coal could be cut anyway. Once NACODS members were going underground with the blessing of NUM, it was possible to keep an eye on the condition of the pit. So when deputies at Abertillery identified some trouble on one of the coalfaces, NUM agreed that some of their members would go underground to sort out the problem. Nobody wanted the pit to sustain damage that might threaten jobs or safety after the strike.

Such an approach was very different from the ethos in Scotland, Notts and Derbyshire, where managements had generally adopted MacGregor's bulldozer approach to industrial relations: crush everything in your path. In Notts, then, relationships between the two unions, and between each union and management, were very different from those in South Wales and Shireoaks. At Bottom Pit in Hucknall, South Notts, with only about 44 strikers out of 1000 NUM members, NACODS crossed picket lines throughout the strike. At Gedling, also in South Notts, the situation was the same. Shot firer Dave Hewitt, a NACODS member there in 1984-5, recalls coal being produced throughout the strike. Dave was unaware until later that NACODS members at some other pits were refusing to cross picket lines, although he believes his union officials must have known but kept it quiet. He thinks that, along with other NACODS members, he received a personal letter from MacGregor, who was fond of going over the heads of union leaders and addressing union members personally. That tactic made miners feel more vulnerable, as well as belittling the unions by ignoring their existence. Prior to MacGregor's reign, management had always communicated with the workforce by talking to the unions.

In autumn 1984 MacGregor in his wisdom decided to force all deputies back to work by refusing to pay them unless they crossed picket lines. NACODS members, already concerned about pit closures, were furious. In a ballot 82% of their members voted to strike, which would by law have stopped all underground operations, including those in the midlands pits that were still producing coal. We were all delighted by the prospect of a swift victory after our members' months of suffering. In those few days of excitement Arthur happened to see me as he walked around National Office. If he had a piece of news he would share it with whoever he bumped into, so that day I was told he had been informed by NACODS General Secretary Peter McNestry that it had suddenly become impossible to contact their President Ken Sampey. It seemed to me that some arm of the state had reached Sampey secretly to wreck the NACODS strike decision that would give us victory.

Ten years later McNestry told journalists Seamas Milne and Keith Harper that a member of NACODS Executive had arranged a further meeting at the Advisory, Conciliation and Arbitration Service without his knowledge. McNestry also said MacGregor had told him that if he (McNestry) changed tack he (MacGregor) would take him round the world and show him how real coal industries were run. McNestry said he told MacGregor to "shove" that offer. Some NACODS leaders told the journalists that the more compliant NACODS officials were offered backhanders, jobs and special pension deals in return for their co-operation over ending their dispute. Just twenty-four hours before their strike was due to begin, the NACODS executive called it off, on the grounds that they had been offered a non-binding independent colliery review procedure before any pit was closed. NACODS gave its members no ballot, no opportunity to ask questions or make comments on that review procedure which seemed so irresistible to their leaders. Ken Sampey was quoted as saying later that they had been "sold a pup", as the modified colliery review procedure accepted by their executive failed to save a single pit over the following ten years.

At Shireoaks the instruction from NACODS Executive for members to work, not strike, was largely ignored by its membership. Only a few NACODS men went underground with the tiny band of NUM scabs, but so few NUM members were working that no coal could be produced in any case. Instead they whiled away their shifts playing cards in the stores. George is proud of the fact that throughout the strike not a single cobble of coal was sent to the surface at Shireoaks. NACODS member Dave Hewitt of Gedling in Notts clearly remembers the disquiet, concern and anger of NACODS members at his pit when they received the instruction to continue working despite the ballot result. As they had been working throughout the strike, their anger was not about the Executive's decision itself, but about the lack of democracy in the way it was reached. Selwyn Lloyd of Abertillery also pointed out to me the lack of democracy in the firm instruction from their executive that, despite their earlier ballot result, they should go underground to work. There were no NUM members breaking the strike at Abertillery until the last few weeks, so the new NACODS instruction made no practical difference. Even in those last few weeks, there were too few NUM strike-breakers to produce any coal, so like Shireoaks, Abertillery produced nothing during the long year of the strike. Unfortunately the situation was very different in some other coalfields. Once NACODS had ordered its men back to work, morale slumped amongst NUM members, officials and our band of staff members at National Office. We had come so close to saving our pits and communities, only to find victory snatched away at the very last moment.

North Derbyshire Inspired by the magnificent SEAM community campaign in County Durham, I suggested late in 1984 to North Derbyshire NUM leaders that we should try to organise a local campaign we named the Community Defence Committee. We produced a local leaflet using some of the slogans and images from the National NUM Coal Not Dole pamphlet that I had written. As too many of our local NUM members were working rather than striking, the leaflet was aimed partly at them. It also called on other workers to combat unemployment by offering solidarity, pointing out that pit closures would wipe out tens of thousands of local jobs in engineering, rail and other industries, as well as in mining. We tried to reach out to more people in our local community, but it seemed to me there were too few of us working in that campaign, all of us with many other responsibilities and all of us too tired to make a real impact. Because of the Government and media onslaught on striking miners, and because of management tactics in pressuring our more isolated members into returning to work, the mining communities of North Derbyshire were painfully divided between those who joined the strike and those who worked. Even today there are brothers, one who was on strike, one who scabbed, who will not speak to each other. There were, though, many groups within North Derbyshire's labour movement who gave magnificent support to miners and their families. The outstanding efforts of both rail unions at Shirebrook have already been mentioned, while the engineering union was very supportive.

Solidarity actions by NUM Although our members were appealing to other workers for support, they were also active in offering solidarity to others. Bolsover NUM Branch had gone to Liverpool to raise funds. According to striker Dennis Clayton they were locked up for displaying their colliery banner on the street there. The positive aspect of their trips to that city was the development of close relationships with GMB members at Cammell Laird shipyard. Those Liverpool shipbuilders gave a great deal of support to our Bolsover miners, but they were also locked in a battle to save their own jobs. When the shipyard workers started an occupation they were barricaded by police, using barbed wire, into an accommodation rig. Striking miner Dennis Clayton went over in answer to a call for support, then found the only way to avoid the police while reaching the occupiers was a dangerous route over a high wall, with the risk of falling into the Mersey if he misjudged his step. Like many miners, the occupiers paid a high price for their attempts to save jobs and local economies. They were imprisoned for thirty days, then dismissed, losing their pensions. Although both shipyard and mining industry struggles were ultimately lost, the friendships formed through that solidarity action were to last many years.

Another instance of grassroots solidarity operating in both directions happened while I was running an NUM national residential course (we called them schools) at Wortley Hall near Barnsley. At the start of the week I had, as always, pointed out to our students that the NUM was paying their wages while they attended, so we needed them to take an active part in the learning process. Partway through the week one of our members from Scotland approached me, saying that a few of them would like to join the *Stockport Messenger* mass picket that night. They hoped I would approve. Now we all knew that the owner of the *Messenger* newspaper was trying to break the print unions there, dismissing strikers, then replacing them with scab labour. Those *Messenger* picket lines were subjected to violent enforcement of the new anti-trade union laws by Thatcher's trusted (but not by us) boys in blue. My response was: "Good for you, but you don't need me to tell you how rough the police are being over there, so be careful. You'll need to be back here and in a fit state to join in with our session tomorrow morning. It's a long drive over the Pennines to Stockport and back."

They agreed, so I wished them luck, privately hoping they wouldn't suffer Kate Adie's fate. A BBC journalist, she had only been observing the Messenger picket line as part of her job when a truncheon-wielding policeman had hit her on the head, with no subsequent protests from the BBC. Although I slept badly, worrying about my students' safety, they returned unharmed in time for our morning session. They saw it simply as a necessary act of solidarity, but it must have been very tiring to drive over there, face the police, drive back overnight and then take part in the course next day. Such support was part of the long tradition of solidarity acts by miners to support the struggles of other workers. In past years Yorkshire miners, led by Arthur Scargill, had shown up at the Grunwick picket lines to support a group of striking workers who were mainly Asian women. Our members had also gone on strike to support nurses who needed better pay.

Newspapers and broadcast media We received little or no support from national mainstream press and broadcasting organisations. Following tradition, those bodies had quickly begun to produce reports favouring the Coal Board and Government case rather than ours, so reporters were not welcomed in pit villages or on picket lines. This became a downward spiral in terms of making our case to the general public. Even when we spoke to the press those comments were not accurately reported. After one NEC meeting Arthur and Peter held a press conference at which I heard Arthur giving a brilliant summary of our case for keeping pits open. Although I was really looking forward to seeing this address broadcast on BBC evening news, his speech was suppressed nearly completely in the bulletin because they devoted almost the whole time to a story about the first scab returning to work in Yorkshire, escorted by large numbers of police officers.

After that we decided to record our press conferences ourselves, with staff member Keith Brookes using our new video camera, so we could prove what was said and compare it with what was shown on TV news. I was astonished by the effect on professional camera crews when we began making our own recordings. In those days, before mobile phones or widespread private ownership of video equipment, broadcasters were used to having a monopoly on filming. Clearly feeling threatened by our use of a video camera, one of them pulled, or perhaps kicked, our camera plug out of its wall socket so I had to make my way through the crush to ram it back in place before we lost too much footage. I showed footage of our press conference to a meeting of our members, following it with the footage that had been shown on national news the same day. They were startled at the difference between what had been said and what had been reported, but as time went on they learned from experience to trust neither TV news nor mainstream newspaper stories.

BBC radio journalist Nicholas Jones admitted in print years later that journalists in mainstream media organisations, including himself, often allowed themselves to be convinced by the Government propaganda machine that some pit closures were being made in order to save the rest of the industry. He pointed out that his earlier naïve belief had left him shocked in the 1990's when Major's Government shut down most of the remaining pits. At that time Government encouraged what was termed the "dash for gas", a switch to gas, which was cheaper than coal, for generating electricity. Afterwards Jones accepted the accusation that as the strike progressed most journalists became, in effect, cheerleaders for "the return to work", which was nothing more than the campaign to pressure more and more miners into breaking the strike. As Jones pointed out, that suited newspaper proprietors such as Rupert Murdoch, who wanted to see the miners defeated because they were already planning onslaughts on trade union organisation within their own newspapers. Many journalists failed to understand that point until it was too late, for both us and them. Although welcome, expressions of regret made years later were of no use once we had lost our battle to save the industry. Left-wing newspapers and journals, acting as antidotes to the poison of right-wing newspapers by reporting the union's case and urging support for our efforts, reached too few people.

International solidarity Miners were always internationalists. If a single miner was killed anywhere in the world our NEC would stand in silence as an act of remembrance, knowing that miners everywhere faced great dangers at work. During that period Arthur Scargill was trying to build an international miners' organisation which would span the divisions created right across the middle of Europe by the Cold War. I remember being at some function attended by Augustin Defresne, known as "Tin Tin", the French miners' leader. Very few of our NUM group could speak another language so I tried to lubricate my rusty schoolgirl French, managing to have a discussion with Tin Tin that included the French practice of using adult learning community development workers called animateurs. While suspecting he would be wincing inwardly at my poor pronunciation, I felt I ought to say something in his language, rather than expecting him to make the effort to speak English all the time.

During the strike many miners' unions and other unions right across the world offered us wonderful solidarity. Throughout the strike Australian dockers refused to load coal that was destined for Britain. At our NEC meeting in December 1984, we heard that Mick McGahey had been present when the TUC General Council hosted a meeting with its sister bodies in Holland, West Germany and Belgium. They discussed how to stop coal imports into Britain, and how to seek further solidarity action. Solidarity gifts for our striking members were coming from across the world, while tins of food were sent from countries right across Europe. This food aid sometimes created problems, though. I heard a number of coalfield women and men saying they had felt unable to use jars of food from Eastern Europe because they could not fathom what was inside. Nobody could read the labels, written in Cyrillic alphabet. John Lander's family were given some glass jars of food from Russia. When they were opened and tasted, he recalls that what was inside neither looked nor tasted pleasant, although they appreciated the good intentions of Russian miners who sent the parcels. The French trades union body CGT sent aid convoys across the Channel, with some of those solidarity goods reaching North Derbyshire. Graham Skinner remembers high-quality children's painting sets arriving in Clay Cross in time for Christmas. John Lander's children in North Derbyshire also received Christmas presents from French trades unionists. The government of the Soviet Union, determined to offer solidarity to the miners, ensured that their mining industry refused to honour its contract to supply coal to Britain during our strike. Regrettably the Polish Government insisted on honouring its contract to supply coal to Britain, despite our pleas.

Solidarity by arts workers Although some key parts of the trade union movement failed to offer the support we needed, many workers in creative fields showed generosity and commitment in their solidarity efforts. Two radical film companies produced *Coal Not Dole, The Miners' Campaign Videotapes*, featuring miners, coalfield women and sympathetic MPs who all explained our case. In those days before social media had been invented, it was hoped that film would become a means of communication that could by-pass official TV news channels and mainstream newspapers. Unfortunately filming and editing took such a long time that it never became a substitute for the immediacy of TV.

Famous folk singers Ewan MacColl and Peggy Seeger wrote and performed songs for a cassette tape, produced at their own expense, which was sold through NUM National Office and other union channels to raise money for the Solidarity Fund. Peggy herself never made use of assistants for that work, instead ringing me in person to discuss arrangements for getting copies of the cassettes distributed. Less-famous performers, with their own local followings, often worked hard in concerts for which they received no money, sending all receipts to the Solidarity Fund or local NUM coffers instead. In South Yorkshire and North Derbyshire, education workers John Young and Ray Hearne formed a double act called The Red Gazunders, performing without fees in benefit concerts at night on top of their day jobs. Many of their songs were self-written. Derbyshire group Flamin' Nerve worked hard in the same way, with group member Mal Finch writing the song "We are women, we are strong, we are fighting for our lives..." Adopted and loved by the women's support groups, this became known to all as The Mining Women's Song. Even years after the strike, joining in when it was sung in Chesterfield Labour Club still reduced me to tears. Many famous artistes performed free of charge at a series of London concerts, named *Five Nights for the Miners*, where all ticket money was donated to the Solidarity Fund.

The need for such support did not wither once the strike had ended because even in 1986 we still had 583 sacked members, including six in prison, whom we were trying to support via the Solidarity Fund. Many of those had been sacked for paltry or trumped-up reasons. After

Monday September 3rd

Dave Kelly Band with
Geno Washington
Alexei Sayle
Rik Mayall
Interval (20 mins)
Loundon Wainwright III

Tuesday September 4th

Bert Jansch Band
Alan Hull.
Interval (20 mins)
Home Service
Dave Swarbrick's
Whippersnapper

Wednesday September 5th

Shakisha
Desmond Johnson
SUS
Interval (20 mins)
No Fixed Address
Daddy Colonel/Tipper Ire/
Phillip Levi
Misty in Roots

Thursday September 6th

Christy Moore
Interval (20 mins)
Van Morrison

Friday September 7th

Andy De La Tour
Working Week
Ben Elton/Andy de la Tour
Mike Harding
Interval (20 mins)
Alexei Sayle
WHAM
Rik Mayall
Some of big country
Nigel Planer
Paul Weller & Mick Talbot

Persons shall not be permitted to stand or sit in any of the gangways intersecting the seating or sit in any of the other gangways.
Members of the public are reminded that no tape recorder or other type of recording apparatus may be brought into the auditorium. It is illegal to record any performance, or part thereof, unless prior arrangements have been made with the General Administrator and concert promoter concerned.

No smoking in the auditorium.

The taking of photographs is not permitted.

First Aid facilities are provided by the British Red Cross Society.

Steinway & Sons supply pianos to the South Bank Concert Hall.

the strike we held an individual ballot, campaigning for a levy of 50p a week to be taken from each member's pay, in order to support those we all called "sacked lads".

At that time there was still a Sacked Miners' Office in the Greenwich Labour Rooms, showing that many Labour Party activists and organisations continued to oppose their Leader's disapproval of the miners' cause. The long-playing record *Heroes* was created in the North East after the strike to raise money that would help the sacked lads and those in prison. The GLC staged a follow-up concert, featuring many of the same artistes, in the Albert Hall. Billy Bragg, Lindisfarne and Alun Armstrong were just a few of the stars who performed once more without fees, raising the huge sum of £25,000 for the Miners Solidarity Fund. The event was more than just a fund-raising entertainment, as Peter Heathfield, Tony Benn, the Chair of the GLC and others all made speeches. That might have been the evening when the National Justice for Mineworkers campaign was launched. As late as March 1987 the Heroes concert was performed in Sheffield to continue raising money for our sacked members. Women Against Pit Closures groups in at least seven coalfields were still organising events for the benefit of sacked miners during that period.

Yet despite the magnificent efforts of so many unions, labour movement organisations, community groups, miners' support groups, performers and individuals, the power of the state, sharpened by Thatcher's Law, defeated our members' heroic efforts. Fatal divisions, sown initially within our own ranks by those such as Notts full-time official Roy Lynk, then financed by David Hart and other government assets, made life much easier for those union leaders who did not want to support the NUM strike. In their extended time of desperate need our striking canteen workers, clerical workers, workshop specialists and miners deserved, but did not receive, overwhelming support from a unified trade union movement.

The consequences of our defeat spread far beyond mining communities, though. Every worker in Britian is still suffering the effects of our loss of the miners' strike, whether in wages, the right to join a trade union, or the right to take industrial action at a time of their choosing. Our only victory lay in the heroic endurance of our striking members and their families, sustained over that long year.

10 Contraband

All miners understand that contraband is the name for forbidden objects. Tobacco, matches or other flammable items must not be taken underground for fear of starting a fire that could lead to disaster. At the start of each shift miners were searched before stepping into the cage that would take them underground. During the strike both sides tried to gain advantage over the other and my choice is to describe these moves as attempts by each side to smuggle contraband past the other.

Police posing as pickets Steve Brunt, then of Arkwright Colliery, now a former Chesterfied Mayor, remembers spotting a man in the street whom he knew to be a policeman, but who seemed to be dressed like a picket. When Steve commented on that, the officer replied that he had not expected to have to wear fancy dress when he'd joined the police force. Posing as pickets, they could pick up information or create trouble on picket lines without anyone realising who they were. That was shown to be happening on a much larger scale, too. Jack Smith, Assistant Area Coal Board Transport Manager in Derbyshire, and a member of management union BACM, worked at the Board's Transport Office, on the road leading to Markham colliery. He told me he would see police officers in uniform being driven in hired buses past his office to collieries, returning dressed as pickets. Police often dossed down in the office where Jack worked, to rest in between more taxing duties. One day in the week beginning 18 June, when Jack went into the office for a night shift, he noticed that the Fleet Engineer looked dreadful. When he asked what the matter was, the engineer, clearly upset, would not talk in front of witnesses, who were police officers, so they took a walk outside. The engineer said he had overheard police officers bragging about having been at Orgreave, dressed up as pickets and throwing stones. Kevin Horne, charged with riot at Orgreave, recognised someone that day he knew had been, and probably still was, a police officer who was dressed as a picket. Such activities showed police had been used as Government contraband, using their disguises to deliberately create trouble. A huge number of genuine pickets were charged with riot at Orgreave on June 18, but of course no police officer has ever been charged over bad conduct at Orgreave.

Thatcher's claim Echoed by mainstream media, one of Thatcher's items of contraband, which was successfully smuggled through to the nation, was her claim that the Coal Board, not her government, was running the strike. Although at the time we knew that was a lie, her deception was only publicly revealed much later, on publication of her political memoir. There she described her own active involvement in the strike. For instance, she wrote about meeting two groups of "working miners". That was the term used by management, Government and the media for those who broke the strike. Within the NUM, we followed trade union tradition and called them scabs. Derbyshire miners seemed to recognise different levels of scabbing. Those who had never joined the strike were called Day One-ers, meaning they had scabbed from day one. You could hear in the tone of voice when miners spoke of them that they were seen as the lowest of the low. Those who returned to work before the strike officially ended were often still called scabs, although as the strike ground on for month after month, many strikers felt that word was not a fair way to describe those who might have returned to work after being out for eight or ten months. This was an issue that caused many NUM members unease, as public shaming and yells of "scab" were one of the few weapons available to striking workers struggling to keep a strike solid, in hope of preserving their communities. Yet even a Derbyshire miner who returned to work after eight months used the word:

"I went in on't scab bus".

Government spying   Another piece of contraband smuggled in by the state was wholesale invasion of our privacy, as well as our right to organise as a trade union. As the strike went on all of us, National Office staff, full-time officials and activists in the coalfields, discovered that our work and home phones seemed strange, with odd echoes on the line. Maurice Jones, editor of *The Miner*, told me it was a sure sign someone was listening in, and that it would be Special Branch or the Security Services. As there were literally thousands of us having our phones tapped, it was impossible to imagine that a Government minister could be authorising each eavesdropping instance, which was supposed to be the official procedure before a phone could be tapped. It was not pleasant to be aware that the state was listening in to all our conversations, even the most intimate conversations unconnected with the strike. We had plenty of proof that police were also using phone tapping to counter our strike organisation. For instance, on duty in the Control Room one day I was contacted by someone in one of the Yorkshire NUM strike centres, asking to speak to Trevor Cave.

"I'm sorry, he's just gone home after a night shift. Can I help?"

"Just give 'im a message, will you?" the voice said. "Tell im to come for breakfast and stay for dinner."

"All right, I'll leave 'im a message."

We all had our own coalfield contacts, and sometimes felt the need to speak in code on the phone. Had I been less tired from night duties and less woolly-minded from taking painkillers for my illness, I might have guessed what this message meant. Instead I put it aside for Trevor and thought no more about it until I bumped into him the following day. He told me the message had been a request for pickets to go early and remain at at one of the Yorkshire pits.

"Of course, no extra pickets arrived because I didn't get the message in time. But you know what? The police turned up in large numbers this morning – they hadn't had many officers there for weeks, but suddenly police flooded into the pit lane. They must have been listening in to the phone call you took yesterday. It's a pity the police came for nothing – there were very few pickets there to meet them."

Our contraband: pickets   The state's mass eavesdropping was coupled with police action that was spurred on by Thatcher's instructions that they must be harder. Such an approach turned our pickets into contraband that we needed to smuggle past the police who, like an occupying army, were denying public access into Nottinghamshire. That should never have been necessary in a country whose Government claimed it was a functioning democracy.

We had to find other secure ways of communicating, which sometimes meant knocking on contacts' doors to avoid using our tapped phones. One bright spring day early in the strike, I found myself knocking on the door of Ida Hackett's flat in Mansfield. A respected community adviser, activist and Communist for decades, she was the accepted leader of all the mining women's support groups that had sprung up throughout the Notts coalfield. She had probably helped form many of them. Ida advised, encouraged and informed, but most of all she inspired the women, the striking miners and the Area officials – at least, those officials who were supporting the strike. Aware of the problem with phones, which she was experiencing herself, Ida had readily agreed to my visit without asking any questions when I had rung her initially. I needed to discuss an idea put to me by Roger Windsor, although I was never sure who had first thought of it. As Ida and I had known and worked with each other for years before the strike began, when we wanted to get something sorted out, we didn't mess about making small talk first. As soon as I had introduced Peter Neilson, the branch official from the Scottish Craftsmen's Area of the NUM who was with me that day, I plunged straight in.

"I need to talk to you about the Mansfield march and rally."

"We're building support for it and we'll make sure there's a good turnout.

Of course Ida had already been working on preparations for that event. I had expected nothing less but needed to break in on her list of what she had already done.

"There's more to it than that, Ida. You know all the trouble we're having getting pickets in from other coalfields because of the police roadblocks. Do you think you could organise accommodation for some lads from other coalfields if they just didn't go home after the rally? They could disappear into the villages and boost the numbers of our pickets for a bit."

Ida didn't hesitate for a moment. Just as I had expected, she started listing names of people who would probably take the undercover pickets into their homes. Peter was impressed.

"If you can sort out some accommodation like this, we could organise some of our boys so they're prepared to stay here in Nottinghamshire for a while, instead of going straight back to Scotland on our buses as soon as the rally ends."

"That's great, Peter. At National, we can use our contacts to get the same arrangements made with pickets from other coalfields."

It was time, then, to start sending discreet messages through to other coalfields, using trusted staff members and our personal contacts. We all knew that no mention of these arrangements should be made on our workplace or home phones, so I was very careful. When asking colleagues if they would use their own contacts in the coalfields to suggest some of our members might stay behind in Notts after the rally I stressed the need for secrecy. While the Miners' March on Mansfield was assembling outside the Civic Centre on that sunny May morning I kept asking over the microphone for stewards from particular Areas of the union to come to the loudspeaker van. All stewards I called had some people on their buses who would not be going home for a while so I needed to use that large gathering as cover to introduce them to Ida, who would put them in touch with their local hosts. Because pickets would no longer need to try "getting over the border" at police roadblocks on M1 Junctions 28 or 29, it would be easier for them to reach the pits where they were needed. So few of our Notts members were on strike that they needed extra help from pickets outside the coalfield. Overnight accommodation with local families would mean pickets could come from Yorkshire, or even as far away as Scotland or the North East, without being turned back at police roadblocks on M1 junctions and even on minor roads.

That Mansfield march on May 14, 1984, attracted such large numbers from many coalfields that I was able to report an attendance of 40,000 people to our Annual Conference. That huge show of support for the strike, in the middle of the largest working coalfield, was impressive. As in Sheffield, I had contracted Highway Scaffolding to erect a high platform floored with wooden boards. This time their worker did not even try to sell me the idea of saving money by not having safety barriers around the edges. Roger and I stayed with the stage at the Leisure Centre car park while everyone else marched around the town. Once they returned and the rally began, lots of people crowded onto the stage, including journalists, for reasons I never understood. Perhaps they thought they would get an extra story by standing near our main speakers Arthur Scargill and Peter Heathfield. As the meeting went on I noticed the platform was beginning to sag beneath our feet. The weight of bodies must be reduced without causing panic, or there could be a nasty accident, so I began to speak in turn very quietly to everyone who did not need to be onstage. Once I had alerted them to the problem and they then noticed the boards sagging, they moved off without a fuss.

That was one problem sorted, but there was another worry too. A group of our younger members had climbed onto a nearby roof to get a better view of the platform. Arthur appealed to them several times to come down off the roof because we were worried it might collapse under the weight of bodies, or one of them might fall. They ignored his pleas. It was strange that some of our younger members were in the habit of chanting "Arthur Scargill walks on water", yet that group ignored his repeated requests that they come off the roof because it was dangerous. Jim Parker and I, standing near Arthur and Peter, were making the muttered asides of the middle-aged that have persisted through the centuries: young people have no respect these days, they won't listen… Fortunately nothing bad happened to our young members on the roof.

Arthur and Peter gave powerful speeches as usual. We had hoped their presence, together with such a large turnout, would encourage more working miners to join the strike but so far as I could tell that did not happen, with the vast majority of Notts miners continuing to work. At the end of the march and rally on May 14 I rode off back to Sheffield in a chartered bus, thinking that the whole day had gone well, with such a huge crowd of marchers from across all our coalfields. In my innocence I believed for thirty-nine years that our plan to smuggle in pickets from other Areas had succeeded. Some members who had arrived in buses for the rally were being spirited into strikers' homes in Notts, rather than making the bus journey home.

I had no idea what was about to happen in the town and surrounding villages. It seems that the police provoked trouble on Chesterfield Road, near where the return coaches were parked. There were also disturbances at the same time in the Market Place. Although some miners fought back, others did nothing but were still arrested. Fifty-five people were charged with affray and riot.

Suspecting each other Then my illusions about the success of our undercover operation were wrecked when researcher Joe Diviney showed me an NUM Area Circular dated 8th May 1984, sent from National Office to Area Secretaries. To my amazement the Circular suggested that after the rally some of our members might stay in Notts until a later date. At first I could not believe what I was seeing, then I spotted Roger Windsor's initials, identifying him as its author. On Roger's instructions I had arranged for the smuggling into Notts of pickets as contraband, while his Area Circular ensured that the same plan became public knowledge at strike centres in every coalfield. Literally hundreds of striking NUM members would have been discussing the plan to smuggle in pickets, using the rally as cover. That meant it was inevitable that the police would hear of it, so they were encouraged to arrest many miners in Mansfield after the march. During the days that followed they also arrested many pickets who were staying with host families in the area. In the month before police attacked pickets at Orgreave, some of those arrested in and around Mansfield were charged with riot then put on trial in Nottingham. That trial has remained almost unknown, although the threat to defendants charged with riot was just as serious as at the Orgreave trial, with defendants also facing possible life imprisonment. My partner Barry Johnson, president of Chesterfield Trades Council and vice-chair of East Midlands TUC, attended the Mansfield riot trial, held in Nottingham, whenever he could, keeping me up to date with what was happening there. Fortunately the defendants in Nottingham, like the Orgreave defendants in Sheffield, were not convicted.

At least one of my colleagues also experienced some odd behaviour by Roger, who told our Research Officer Dave Feickert that he had purchased an off-the-shelf company called Oakedge. He said that would enable us to buy and safeguard some NUM office equipment in case the Receiver sent people in to take away our stuff. Dave, following an instruction from Roger, took home a computer Roger told him belonged to this little company, so it would remain available to us whatever else the receiver might seize. Soon afterwards he was astonished to find Roger had informed Arthur Scargill that the computer was missing, presumed stolen. Totally honest, as well as devoted to the NUM, Dave would never have stolen anything, yet he was forced to explain to Scargill that the "stolen" computer was in fact in his own home.

Circumstances at the time led us to suspect each other when there was any adverse publicity beyond the normal distortions of the mainstream media. We understood that the security services had rented offices nearby from which they were photographing our National Office, so Arthur always kept his office blinds drawn. It was also known that the security services were boasting of having "indirect but reliable" contacts with members of the NUM National Executive. I regularly tormented myself by wondering which of my colleagues might be talking to security services agents, or might themselves be agents, of the state whose Prime Minister had vilified us as "the enemy within" We now know that Stella Rimington, later to become head of MI5, was officially in charge of an MI5 team that was watching us.

Labour Party/TUC liaison meeting Roger Windsor called me into his office one day to tell me that the Labour Party had called a Labour/Trades Union Liaison meeting in London. I had to squash the cynical thought that, with a General Election on the horizon, of course the Labour Party would have suddenly remembered the unions. Our Head of Administration Trevor Cave was the person responsible for our relations with the Labour Party, so I was struggling to understand why Roger was talking to me about this.

"We need to be represented at this meeting, but Trevor's unavoidably absent and I can't make the date, so I want you to go instead."

"But Roger, you know I'm a member of the Communist Party – surely it wouldn't be a good idea for me to go to a Labour Party TUC Liaison meeting."

"We have to have a presence at this meeting, and you're the only person free to go. Everyone will assume that you're a Labour Party member."

"But it seems so underhand, and what if there's someone there who knows about my Communist Party membership, or if it comes out afterwards? It could be made to look as though the NUM was trying to sabotage the meeting in some way, or as though the Communist Party was trying to infiltrate the Labour Party, with the help of the NUM. It could cause us a lot of embarrassment."

"Don't worry, it'll be all right. You're the only one who can go on that day, and it's only the once."

Clearly his mind was made up, and as he'd instructed me to go, I didn't see that I had any other choice. As both National Officials were away, I couldn't even try going over Roger's head by informing them of his instruction, so I was forced to show up, then try to be as helpful as possible without being conspicuous. Roger had forced me into attending that Labour Party Trade Union Liaison meeting under false pretences: he had turned me into an item of contraband that we were smuggling past the Labour Party and the trades unions. If the story had come out, I would have been unable to defend myself in public because National Office staff were strictly prohibited from speaking to the press. I was also very unhappy that I had been forced into that false position within the labour movement.

"Silver Birch" Thatcher, aided by the compliant mainstream media, was in full strident cry. She and they never stopped accusing the NUM of a lack of democracy, despite the decision of participants in our Special Delegate Conference on April 19, 1984 to support the strike. Various Notts working miners, such as the self-styled Silver Birch, also attacked us for lack of democracy. It was too easy to think, as I did, that he was probably acting as an agent of the state. Yet that was later proven accurate, when journalist Solomon Hughes of the *Morning Star* used a Freedom of Information inquiry. He discovered that a police report to the Home Secretary indicated Silver Birch reported during the strike to a detective inspector in the Intelligence office at Nottinghamshire Police Headquarters. The police apparently thought he was not too bright and did not have much effect on miners, although he was lauded in the national press. Silver Birch's enthusiasm, though, remained undimmed over many years, as he used an interview for the Channel 4 documentary in 2024 to repeat the accusation of lack of NUM democracy under the left-wing leadership of the 1980's. That was quite a cheeky accusation for a man to make when he himself was reporting his fellow-workers and his own union to undercover police officers. He was another item of Government contraband.

Roger Windsor meets Gadaffi There have always been unanswered questions about the damaging publicity surrounding Roger Windsor's trip to Libya. Because of the earlier murder in a London street of PC Yvonne Fletcher by someone shooting from inside the Libyan embassy, Libya was regarded with disgust by many people in Britain.

Newspapers implied that Roger had been spotted by chance at the airport as he was travelling, which seems unlikely as he was not well-known until after that story was splashed across the Sunday Times. Roger said later that, once he had arrived at Gaddafi's headquarters, an aide had taken and released photographs of his public embrace with Gadaffi. However, that would not have explained how British newspaper scouts had apparently known enough to recognise and photograph Roger at an airport, unless the Libyans had tipped off the *Sunday Times*. Although it was claimed that Roger had travelled to Libya to ask for money from Gaddafi, I always thought it more likely that the NUM was hoping to hide money out of the reach of the British Government. The story burst into public view just a few days after the NUM's funds had been sequestrated, or taken out of our reach. It was an extremely convenient moment for the British Government, as it distracted the media, and therefore the public, from the state's hostile act against our union. I assumed that Arthur Scargill had sent Roger to Libya, particularly as he never denied prior knowledge of the trip. Peter Heathfield said in my hearing that he had not known about Roger's journey until he read it in the papers, and I knew Peter was an honest man. Mick McGahey also said that he had not known beforehand. I have wondered if Roger could have made that trip on his own initiative. Roger's visit to Libya was an episode that made it even harder for the NUM to get a fair hearing from the news media in Britain.

David Hart We knew that Thatcher's unofficial, and therefore deniable, asset David Hart functioned as contraband smuggled in by Government. He seemed to be what a Tory politician of the time called "one of the Downing Street irregulars", answerable only to Thatcher. Thought to have links with both British and US Security Services, he was said to use a chauffeur-driven Mercedes to travel the coalfields. Hart fomented and funded dissent, strikebreaking and legal cases taken out by NUM members against their own union. In between those forays he stayed in luxury at Claridge's hotel in London. Compare his lifestyle with that of our striking members who, deep in debt because they had no wages, were cold and hungry, short of shoes and clothes. Worse still, they could see their children suffering the same hardship. I could never understand why so many working miners seemed to believe Hart was trying to help, rather than trying to use them.

Although I never had personal contact with Hart he was well known to some of the working miners in the Notts coalfield because he gave money to both Notts and National Working Miners' Committees. Many working miners, as Labour supporters and members, felt very uneasy about that because they understood such donations were coming from Tories. Such discomfort led to an appeal by Bentinck Branch to Notts Area Council in November 1984, urging the Area to dissociate itself from both Working Miners' Committees. Area Council did just that. David Amos, a leading working miner and branch official from Newstead pit, told me that in January 1985 he attended a Notts Area weekend school where he encountered Colin Clarke. Clarke, a delegate to Area Council from a different pit, was still involved with both Working Miners' Committees, despite the Area Council decision to break off relations with them. David Amos asked him about the donors who were funding those bodies, and what amounts were involved. The response was bitter:

"I'll just remind you that you have broken ties with the Working Miners' Committees and that is my business and none of yours."

Secret imports of Libyan oil Another example of Government contraband was only revealed to us in the summer of 1985. We were surprised to hear Jim Slater, general secretary of the National Union of Seamen, using his fraternal address to our NUM Annual Conference to tell us of another example of Government contraband. He said that the Government and Central Electricity Generating Board, a huge customer of British Coal, had conspired to import Libyan oil worth £150 million in order to undermine our strike. The ship carrying that oil spent a single night in a European port in order to hide the origin of its cargo. Yet over that same period the NUM had been attacked bitterly by Government and mainstream media for sending a staff member to Libya for a meeting with Gaddafi.

Over the forty years since the strike, more and more Government papers have been made public, sometimes following investigations by journalists and researchers. Every one of these revelations has confirmed our suspicions that Government ministers, from Prime Minister Thatcher downwards, lied and lied when they claimed they were not interfering in the strike. There now seems to be evidence that the US National Security Agency was also used to intercept our communications, so it seems that Government contraband even included the American state. Our Government was certainly able to smuggle in resources of contraband that dwarfed ours.

11 Decision time

Final Special Delegate Conference of the strike March 3, 1985 Throughout the strike the government had been scuppering attempted negotiations between NUM and Coal Board. In the early months of 1985 our National Executive was focused entirely on trying to reach an agreement that would end the strike. However the Board was no longer even pretending to sit down to negotiate with our officials. It was never clear to me whether that was because they knew whatever they tried to agree would again be wrecked by the government, or because MacGregor himself did not want to negotiate. His wrecking-ball approach to industrial relations never varied. The Board had presented a document to the TUC, to be passed to the NUM, effectively calling for our complete surrender. TUC leaders had been severely embarrassed by the terms of this Coal Board document. Indeed, I remember hearing our National Officials telling our NEC that TUC officers had asked them to stress that they did not support the Coal Board's document, but were simply acting as go-between in passing it to the NUM. This point has not always been understood.

In the period leading up to that last agonising Special Conference, morale among National Office staff had crumbled, along with that in the coalfields. As support for the strike was dropping further every week, I felt desperately low and hopeless, while the faces of other staff members showed similar pain. Surely all those sacrifices made by miners and their families for a year and a half would not end in defeat? We all understood that if we lost the strike, the entire coal industry could soon be shut down or privatised. It was clear, though, that the strike was now unwinnable.

On the morning of that terrible Special Conference, I must have been staying in one of the modest London hotels we used, but I have no memory of anything until, carrying my overnight bag, I stepped wearily into the entrance hall of Congress House, headquarters of the TUC, who had loaned us two rooms for the occasion. To my surprise I spotted Stan Greaves, a senior staff member in the TUC Education Department, together with a colleague. They were leaning on radiators by the window, watching the ever-growing crowd outside.

"Hello, Stan, I didn't expect to see you here today."

"We came to show our support. Is there anything we can do to help?" he asked anxiously.

They had travelled into London on a Sunday just to show their solidarity. Touched by that, all I could manage to say was "Thanks, Stan, but there's nothing anyone can do."

No more words would come.

The NCB had not accepted the Union's offer, agreed at our February 1985 Delegate Conference, to negotiate without any preconditions. The Board would only negotiate if the NUM undertook in advance to discuss "uneconomic pits". A more honest way of putting this would be to say the NUM would have to abandon the whole principle of our strike before the Board would sit down to another negotiating meeting. At that time I was unaware that several Areas had just written letters to Peter Heathfield demanding an end to the strike. In this desperate situation, then, the NEC agreed to call another Special Conference on Sunday 3 March, inviting Areas to submit motions to the NEC beforehand. At National Office we heard that several NUM branches in Yorkshire had told their Area officials that, unless the strike was ended by the Special Conference, they would return to work as whole branches the following week. It appeared that either Special Conference would decide to end the strike or it would collapse anyway, but the problem was more complicated than that, as we shall see. Cumberland, Leicestershire, Nottingham and South Derbyshire Areas had all boycotted this conference – an indication of their disdain for the strike, which very few members in those Areas had ever joined. That meant the small numbers of loyal strikers in those areas had no voice at Conference.

NEC met before the start of Conference to consider motions submitted by Areas. President Arthur Scargill opened that meeting by telling members

"Under Rule the Executive are bound by the previous decision of the Special Conference and therefore in communicating a view on the motions to hand must be obliged to recommend in line with existing policy."

His ruling meant that the National Executive could support none of the area motions unless they echoed the decision of the February Conference to continue the strike without any qualifications. There were three problems with Arthur's ruling. Firstly, previous Conference decisions to fight on had been reached when there was still a bit of hope that the Union could get something out of the Coal Board, which was being controlled by the Government. By early March, though, there seemed no hope of winning anything, with Coal Board figures showing more miners returning to work every week. Although we did not accept the Board's "back-to-work" figures, media outlets published them as gospel truth, so our members as well as the general public tended to believe them. Our own figures indicated that, even including miners off work sick or injured, overall only 60% of miners were not at work. The situation, then, had continued to deteriorate since the previous Conference in February. The second problem was that Scargill's ruling was not the only possible interpretation of the principle that Conference was the supreme decision-making body. There was no principled reason why NEC should not consider the Area motions for which they had called, take a view on each motion, then make recommendations to Conference about a course of action. Conference would remain supreme by either accepting or rejecting the NEC's advice. Scargill's ruling meant that under his presidency, the NEC did not recommend an end to the strike, so no-one could ever accuse him of capitulation. The third problem arising out of his ruling was that Conference delegates, facing agonising decisions, had been looking in vain to the National Officials and NEC for leadership. As no NEC member challenged Arthur Scargill's ruling, the NEC was committed to putting the Area motions to Conference without a specific recommendation. The President would explain to Conference that they were already committed to previous conference decisions. The NEC went to Special Conference, then, offering no leadership apart from a reminder of their commitment to the previous Conference decision to continue the strike.

Once Special Delegate Conference began it was powered by several strong emotions. The first was anger at the lack of leadership from the NEC. Des Dutfield of South Wales said: "What the National Executive have done this morning is a complete abrogation of their responsibility to those boys who have fought for twelve months....We would ask the National Executive again to reconsider that situation. They should have the guts this morning to make a recommendation......."

Scargill returned fire: ... "I submit respectfully that had Areas not been in a position of going public about certain courses of action contrary to the National Union policy we may not have been in the position we are in today."

He was referring to calls made from South Wales for return to work without a settlement, despite previous Conference decisions to continue the strike. I could not help feeling that Arthur was correct there. Over that recent period I had been startled, then very annoyed, to hear Kim Howells make several of those calls on television. Howells, as an appointed staff member, should not have been making any policy statements in public because only elected Area representatives had the right to do that. As South Wales elected officials George Rees and Emlyn Williams had not stopped those public calls by Howells, I believed they were using him as their mouthpiece. Scargill continued: "...The fact is that the National Executive are already mandated. A previous Conference has given an instruction, and that instruction is binding upon the National Executive. The only people who can change that instruction are this Conference itself."

Sammy Thompson of Yorkshire also criticised lack of leadership on the part of NEC, urging: "The NEC should come out with a decision...You should re-meet and take a decision and recommend to this Conference."

So the NEC met again. Even at that second meeting, after some motions had been withdrawn, every remaining Area motion was either rejected or the vote was tied. As President, Arthur Scargill had the power to use a casting vote, but he did not do so on that day, in fact I cannot recall that he ever used his casting vote. So the NEC returned to Delegate Conference unable to offer the lead for which some delegates had called. All remaining Area motions were then open for discussion and decision by Conference.

All delegates who spoke were struck by the gravity of the situation facing us. George Bolton of Scotland said: "We are in the most difficult, most complicated and most dangerous situation we have ever faced in my lifetime in this union."

Many other delegates made similar points. They also seemed driven by fear for both the immediate and longer-term future of the union. Terry Thomas of South Wales, which had been the most solid Area throughout the year of the strike, said: "The one thing that has become obvious to all of us is that the drift back to work is such that we are losing control of the situation. I am saying now I do not believe that the members in South Wales, or indeed in any other Area of the British Coalfield, should have the loyalty they have shown this union abused by allowing this union to be destroyed...The men are calling for leadership, and you have two alternatives. You either give them leadership and repay the loyalty they have given us, or you sit back with your blindfold on and you let the strike collapse around you. That is not leadership."

Of course his comments were correct, but I would have felt less conflicted about them had they not come from South Wales, whose leadership had been personally critical of, and hostile to, the national leadership for months. Other delegates on March 3 made points echoing those of Terry Thomas.

Tommy Callan of Durham spoke of the falling number of strikers in Durham, telling us that in the big collieries two-thirds of the membership were back at work, although they had expelled nearly 200 of their members for returning to work, with another 40 in the pipeline:

"We have nothing left. We are scratching all over."

Billy Etherington of Durham Mechanics explained: "We had a Delegate meeting on Saturday, and there was not one delegate in favour of continuing on with the dispute."

He continued by saying there had been a motion at that meeting for a return to work "And we had to beg from the platform to at least let us come here today and try and get an orderly National return to work so they could possibly go back later next week."

Another delegate said: "After being at different Branch Meetings over the last couple of weeks throughout the country for the Cokemen's Area, it is quite clear the Cokemen's Area have had enough... If we don't lead the men back to work they will go back on their own."

John Burrows of Derbyshire told Conference: "We have been for the for the last five months in the very position that South Wales now fear... We have got to recognise that the grass has been mown down in front of us. There is no cover left. It is no good anybody looking for somewhere to run and hide. There is nowhere left to hide. We have got to take our members back to work. That does not answer all our problems...but at least in taking them back to work we're in control of the situation. If we renege on that responsibility today it will take control of us, because the return to work will come with or without our leadership."

Another strong emotion driving delegates was the sense of responsibility to our hundreds of sacked members, with all motions recognising the urgent need to win back their jobs. That did not necessarily mean staying on strike, though.

John Burrows told us about one of their branch presidents who had been sacked for taking over the headgear and stopping people from going down the pit: "At the branch meeting that was called to decide on our policy in Derbyshire he appealed to his members not to stop on strike in order to retain his job, because he recognised that we can best retain his job and get his work back by being in control of the situation inside. That has happened with other people as well."

Terry Thomas of South Wales made a similar point, while George Bolton pointed out that in their Scottish Area: "You are sacked for any offence of any kind... Wheeler said categorically, over his dead body will they re-start a single sacked miner in Scotland."

He went on to call for: "An enormous national campaign appealing to British people, to this nation, in the name of humanity, decency and justice, to the Churches, political parties, the whole Movement... we can raise such an outcry of Britain's people against the Board and the Government we can force that amnesty."

That was the only concrete proposal for achieving the reinstatement of our sacked members, although unfortunately no such outcry of Britain's people occurred to force the amnesty we needed.

The determination to assist our imprisoned members was another strong emotion voiced by delegates. One of the harshest aspects of Thatcher's Law was the mass criminalisation of miners. Personally I knew Brian Martin and Keith Millward of Clay Cross, both serving sentences for something they had not done, but some of our imprisoned members had indeed committed offences.

Tommy Callan of Durham spoke of: "A young lad that turned a car over. He couldn't do it on his own, but he took the rap. He didn't grass, yet he was sent down for four months...It was the manager's car, by the way (laughter from delegates)... That lad... is going to be protected."

Tommy was looking ahead to the process of negotiation that would hopefully win back the young miner's job in due course. The Midlands delegate spoke about some of his members who had been given five-year sentences: "…Where the lads were trying to stop buses going in, and did a little bit of arson, round about £125,000 worth."

Those buses had been parked in the depot, empty of passengers at the time.

There were also two young miners who had dropped a concrete block from a bridge onto a road when a taxi carrying one of the few Welsh scabs had been travelling below. To everyone's horror the taxi driver had been killed, so our members were in prison on remand, facing murder charges. As everyone anticipated they could be sentenced to many years in prison, Terry Thomas pointed out to Conference that it would be unrealistic to stay out on strike until the union had won amnesty for them. There was great concern for their situation.

I felt that the over-riding emotion amongst delegates that day was despair. There was no possible course of action that was palatable: it was a matter of trying to decide which was the lesser of several evils when Area motions were put to the vote. The South Wales motion had included a call for national negotiations with the Coal Board on amnesty for our sacked lads, but its mover had accepted Arthur Scargill's statement that the Coal Board would not discuss that issue at national level. Only the South Wales motion, urging a return to work without a written settlement, received a majority of votes: 98 for, 91 against. Arthur Scargill then put to Conference a motion from the National Executive, urging delegates to instruct them to set up a Hardship, Victimisation and Benevolent Fund to support members in difficulty at that time and in the future. The proposal was agreed. Arthur then described the Conference as one of the most difficult, if not the most difficult in the history of the National Union of Mineworkers.

He pointed out: "We have not been fighting the Coal Board. We are fighting the Board, the Government, the Police, the judiciary, the media, as they seek to destroy not only sections of our industry but seek to destroy this Union, and with it effective trade unionism in Britain… They have not yet understood that they cannot imprison a mind or sequestrate an idea."

There was nothing more to be said now that could possibly make any difference, or make any of us feel better. Delegates and staff seemed to melt away quickly for their trains, but I needed to wait for a lift promised by a friend. I wandered miserably out into the crowd of demonstrators and supporters, some of them clearly miners and coalfield women, all of them very unhappy. From time to time the word "Scab!" was yelled – without any purpose or justification, I thought. Every so often I could feel tears running down my face. I was not alone in this – there were men and women in the crowd who were also weeping. John Dobb, one of the Notts strike stalwarts who called themselves "Loyal to the Last", remembers that he too cried. At one point a tall, friendly man at the front of the crowd said quietly to me

"It's a great pity, and its effects will last for years".

As we chatted and swapped names, I found he was Francis Koo, general secretary of the charity War on Want, which did valuable anti-poverty work based on a political understanding of its causes. I felt glad that someone outside the trade union movement could understand the lasting nature of our defeat, with its effects still continuing to this day.

Gradually the crowd drifted away while I was still waiting for my lift. Exhausted and anguished, I finally felt able to sink down onto my overnight case to rest. After a while a police officer approached me, making me wonder to myself whether sitting on a suitcase outside Congress House had been made illegal while I wasn't looking. This officer, though, had a different agenda. He began by asking if I was all right, then went on to ask if I had somewhere to stay for the night. He seemed to think that sitting on my case, looking dejected, might mean I was homeless. I assured him that everything was all right and that I was just waiting to be collected by friends. As he went off with his conscience satisfied, I could see a sort of twisted humour in the situation. Only a few months ago the police had stopped me as I visited a picket line at Newstead in Notts. Phoning their headquarters, they had found me on record as having previously been spotted visiting picket lines, proof that they had regarded me as a suspicious person whose movements must be noted and recorded. Today they were taking pity on me. This was an aspect of defeat I had not anticipated.

When my friend and my partner finally arrived with a car, they were sympathetic about the loss of the strike. Yet I felt very lonely during that long journey home, because it seemed that only those who had endured the strike could fully understand the enormity of the exhaustion and grief that we and our members really felt at its final moment of defeat. Typing these words forty years later, those emotions are still as raw. No wonder that even now I feel close to anyone I know, or even meet, who endured the strike.

12 MacGregor's Law

Nicholas Ridley, whose large family fortune had been built, literally, on the backs of miners in the North East, was an ultra-right ideologue who worked with others to formulate what became known as the Ridley Plan, a playbook for picking a nationalised industry and destroying its unions as a prelude to privatisation. Since nationalisation of the coal industry a whole system of consultative committees had been developed, through which the NUM negotiated with management. Many national NCB and local pit managers had worked in the industry, often coming themselves from coalfield communities, so they did not regard miners and their families as beings apart. Ian MacGregor was different, which seemed to be the reason he weas appointed by Margaret Thatcher in 1983 as the new National Coal Board Chairman. He was known for union-busting in the US.

Coal Board Area Managers Once the strike was under way MacGregor's malign influence, Thatcher's unrelenting demonization of the miners, with enthusiastic collusion by TV and newspapers, changed the mood. Many local managers were induced to abandon any former sense of connection with their mining communities. For instance, Ken Moses had been a faceworker at Bold Colliery in Lancashire, but by 1984 he had become the Coal Board's Area Manager for North Derbyshire. Here the NUM individual ballot vote was against strike action, but only by a few votes. Steve Brunt of Arkwright Colliery remembers joining a lobby of several hundred members. Following NUM tradition, they gathered outside the offices before a Derbyshire NUM Area Council meeting, calling for strike action. Area Council agreed to support the strike.

Moses, aware of the almost even division of opinion for and against the strike in his Area, instructed his staff to plot striking miners' addresses on the map to identify those who lived furthest from other miners and strike centres where they could get advice, food parcels and social support. He then focused on breaking the will of those isolated men, or women, by instructing managers to phone or visit their homes, applying pressure to return to work. As the strike progressed, North Derbyshire Coal Board management seemed to expand their bullying operations to include others who were not isolated. John Lander, employed at Duckmanton workshops near Chesterfield, received two or three phone calls from one of his managers, whose name John still remembers forty years later. The manager asked him if he hadn't had enough of the strike, then increased the emotional blackmail by suggesting that if he broke the strike he'd be able to put food on the table for his family. John, knowing his best hope of defending his family was to support the strike in defence of the industry and its jobs, resisted that management pressure. Area official John Burrows recalls standing outside the home of a North Derbyshire miner, watching a management representative inside the man's home trying to browbeat him into returning to work. Many years later John recalled "…and then I explained to the miner why he should not cross the picket line, and where he should go to get help. I also "explained" a few things to the Manager. I'm told he didn't visit any more houses after that." Each miner who succumbed was labelled a scab by his workmates – a lifelong taint. Did Moses ever give a thought to the damage his tactics inflicted on those miners and their communities? As the number of working miners was built up it became easier to persuade more and more NUM members, including canteen staff, to return to work, splitting their communities in ways that have never been repaired. Such tremendous social damage to whole mining communities did not seem to trouble Moses, who was promoted to be the National Coal Board's Technical Director by 1985.

Scottish Area Director Bert Wheeler trod a similar path, ensuring the sacking of more than two hundred miners during the strike. He was loathed by Scottish miners for his bullying tactics. Three cases in particular sparked public anger, when miners convicted in court of minor breaches of the peace, one being fined as little as £25, were dismissed from their jobs. In one notorious incident, managers arranged for a line to be painted on a public road leading to one Scottish pit. Strikers were told that if they stepped over the line they would be sacked, which is exactly what happened. A survey undertaken by our Industrial Relations Department showed our union activists had been a particular target for sackings in Scotland, as 86 men, or 40% of our sacked members there, were branch officials. The Kent Area Secretary reported similar targeting of branch officials in his coalfield. Scottish Area NCB sacked many more members than any other Area. Across all the coalfields more than 960 of our members had been sacked by the end of the strike.

Anger at Wheeler's behaviour was not confined to our union members, as his harsh rule, ending with refusal after the strike to reinstate or even re-engage a single sacked miner, led the churches in Scotland to protest formally to the Coal Board about his behaviour. Dunfermline Council also agreed unanimously to write to the Board, deploring Wheeler's attitude. Such complaints were followed by a summons for MacGregor to appear before a Committee of MPs for questioning. MacGregor took Wheeler to Parliament with him, but as neither of them really budged under questioning, no practical improvement followed. That community anger did no damage to Wheeler's career under MacGregor's rule. In 1985 he was moved to the Area Director's post in South Nottinghamshire, where our members felt his regime like cold showers on their backs. MacGregor had also got rid of the National Coal Board's head of industrial relations and head of public relations because neither Ned Smith nor Geoff Kirk shared MacGregor's view of the miners as simply objects to be used or discarded, depending on which action suited the Coal Board's bottom line and Government determination to privatise the industry. Wheeler, who fitted in with MacGregor's ideal of aggressive management, eventually shared the post of Deputy Chairman of the Coal Board with Ken Moses in 1992.

Returning to the strike period in 1984, we find that tremendous pressure was being exerted nationally by the Coal Board, working with Thatcher and her assistants. Sending letters directly to our members' homes rather than communicating through the NUM, they offered a large Christmas bonus to any miner who returned to work by November 19. Although Thatcher claimed at the time that Government was not involved, her memoir revealed that she and MacGregor worked closely together on that bribe. Her memoir, then, admitted that as Prime Minister she had lied to the country. Adding this offer to North Derbyshire Area Coal Board's tactic of identifying and visiting striking miners to apply pressure, it was not surprising that the most significant return to work was in North Derbyshire. Even some of our members at Arkwright pit, who had stayed solid until then, began to return to work at that point. Only 97 of our members there, a very small proportion, manged to stay out until the end of the strike in March 1985.

In Nottinghamshire the strike never really took hold amongst the majority of miners, so heroic sacrifices were made by the small number of strikers there, who were often stigmatised by their communities. The sheer number of working miners in Notts, Leicestershire and South Derbyshire, though, meant that enough coal was produced to keep power stations running. In at least one Nottinghamshire pit production was recorded as being unaffected by the strike after June 1984.

That continued coal production, the failure of NACODS Executive to carry out the strike for which their members had voted, and the failure of TUC leadership to mount effective action, meant that we lost our battle to save the industry. Our Special Delegate Conference of March 3, 1985 decided by a small margin to return to work without a settlement. As the Coal Board, manipulated by the government, was refusing to negotiate with us, we secured no agreement to win back the jobs of our sacked members. Although our official date of return to work was agreed as Tuesday March 5, the end of the strike was in reality more ragged. That mirrored both its beginning and its formal status, according to the NUM Rulebook, as a series of Area strikes.

Once our members were returning MacGregor was quick to taunt us, writing in the Sunday Telegraph on March 10 1985: "People are now discovering the price of insubordination and insurrection. And boy are we going to make it stick."

That comment illustrates the contempt in which MacGregor held the miners and their communities, as well as his reactionary approach to politics and industrial relations. MacGregor's Law became even harsher after the strike ended.

Sometimes groups of our members refused to return immediately. Some Areas such as Kent refused to go back on the date suggested after the Delegate Conference in March 1985, citing the injustice against sacked mineworkers, so they mounted a picket in Yorkshire. Miners confronted with that picket refused to cross it. John Dobb was one of the minority of miners in Nottinghamshire who went out on strike in 1984-5, supporting their union for the whole year. When he had visited one of the local sacked lads and seen the poor conditions in which he and his family were living, John had been deeply upset. He operated on the principle that you never left your wounded on the battlefield, which is why he was horrified when Special Delegate Conference decided to return to work in March 1985 without having won back the jobs of our many sacked members. John and another Hucknall miner stayed out beyond the nationally-determined day of the return to work.

"We couldn't bear to go back while there were still lads who'd been sacked and lads who were in prison."

After a fortnight the union man said management would sack them unless they went back, so they were forced to return. When John turned up for his first shift on nights at Hucknall's "Bottom Pit", none of the other miners would speak to him because they had all been scabbing. Underground, poor relationships can be dangerous because they can threaten safety.

In that fraught situation the overman was not sure what to do with him, so: "He put me on a button in the middle of nowhere".

On that first shift, then, John saw nobody. Being a "button man", whose job underground was to press a button at certain times, was a low-status job within the underground workforce. John had previously done a very high-status job as a faceworker and chargeman who drove the shearer, the machine that cut coal. On John's second shift, the overman said he had put together a scratch team for care and maintenance work on the Thirty Ones seam that was to be kept for emergency use in case of breakdown on other seams. Would John do him a favour by driving for him on Thirty Ones? Most members of that team had been strikers. Later, someone named this team the Leper Colony and the name stuck. All the ex-strikers ignored that name.

John remembers: "A lot of the scabs were more curious about us than anything. Most men at Hucknall wanted to talk to the strikers. A lot of the scabs on my shift were just sheep".

When the Thirty Ones face shut, John was invited onto another team until Bottom Pit was shut with almost no notice. The men were told to make a list of other pits where they would like to work. All his team, except for John, were moved to Thoresby, but those who had been on strike were not allowed into Thoresby. John said he would like to go to Ollerton, but one of the managers said he himself was moving to Ollerton, and: "There's too many of your sort there already."

That jibe referred only to John's status as one of the few "Loyal to the Last" strikers in 1984-5. He had also been elected NUM Branch President at Bottom pit when the NUM branch was re-formed following breakaway by UDM.

"I ended up at Sherwood."

Life there was very tough for NUM members, who were in a minority. Denied all workplace union facilities, they were forced to conduct an NUM ballot in a member's front room because they were not allowed facilities to do this at the pit.

"Some men were sacked just for talking in the canteen – they were accused of having a union meeting in there, which wasn't true. I was attacked in t'pit yard by a scab, so I flattened him. I only got a final written warning for that – don't know why I wasn't sacked."

John would not say this, but he was known to others as a hard-working miner, so perhaps that was why he was not dismissed. Working at Sherwood until it too closed, John remembers bitterly: "There was no justice – it was the Wild West."

The Wild West also operated at Bolsover colliery. On their first day back after the strike, Dennis Clayton and workmates found that their boots had become unfit to wear after a year in storage, so they were waiting to be issued with new footwear and clothing by the storeman. A manager tapped on the window, falsely accused them of holding an NUM meeting there, while telling them such meetings were forbidden from then on. Only the breakaway UDM was to be tolerated at Bolsover. Over time, the NUM branch put as much pressure as possible on management, seeking recognition as before. Eventually they were told that if they became the majority union at Bolsover, management would recognise the NUM and resume negotiations. For a long time branch officials worked hard until they had recruited more members than the UDM, then they approached management for the promised recognition. Management refused to honour its promise, so the NUM had no negotiating rights and no facilities for conducting union business. At one point Bolsover NUM branch officers were forced to conduct a union ballot in a nearby bus shelter because the UDM were occupying their former union office. Management operated such blatant discrimination between NUM and UDM that our 1986 National Conference received reports of higher wages being paid to UDM members, compared to NUM members, in Ellistown in Leicester, at some pits in Durham, Lancashire and North Derbyshire.

Another example of this new Wild West came from Calverton in South Notts Area. At a time when miners were seeking transfers as their own pits closed, one NUM member was told by the UDM, the only body recognised by management there, that he would not be allowed to work at Calverton unless he joined their organisation and signed a document to say that he would never rejoin the NUM. Colliery management was allowing the UDM to select its workforce. That was all part of the Coal Board's drive to destroy the NUM in Notts by building up the UDM.

Another example of the Wild West in the new territory created by Macgregor's Law came in the treatment of Dennis Clayton at Bolsover. In the early 1990's, several years after the end of the strike, he went to work one Monday morning to find a letter with his check. Checks were the tokens that miners showed to draw their pay. Another check was also carried underground, so in case of accident each man could be identified. This letter instructed Dennis to see a Mr Wallace from Personnel, who then told him it was time to take redundancy.

"I didn't go on strike for a year so I could take redundancy now", Dennis protested. He was shocked by Mr Wallace's response.

"Management want rid of union activists like you. You'd do better to take redundancy, with its payment, because they'll do anything to sack you, then you'd have nothing. Why not go home and talk it over with your wife, then come back and let me know what you decide?"

Dennis didn't want to give up his job, but life at the pit had been a lot worse since the end of the strike. He was having to work with UDM members who had scabbed, so after a serious talk with his wife: "I decided to go for it. If management really wanted rid of me, they'd be able to get away with any excuse for sacking me, then I'd have nothing.

Back in Mr Wallace's office next day, he had only one bargaining tool.

"I did twelve years at Williamthorpe, but it's not on my record, so my redundancy pay wouldn't include those years of service. I won't take redundancy unless those years are put on my record."

Mr Wallace agreed that the record would be adjusted, so Dennis won his point. The Coal Board agreed to pay the five rest days he had left. After confirming his willingness to take redundancy, then signing a document, he expected to be given the usual two weeks of notice. To his amazement, he was told that his employment had just ended.

"My head was spinning. I'd no time to get used to the idea of never going back down the pit, no chance to say goodbye to my workmates."

Dennis was told he could keep his checks, then he must leave the premises immediately. He found it hard to adjust to this abrupt change in his life. Once he completely forgot he no longer had a job.

"I'd been a chargeman and done a lot of overtime. Sometimes I'd worked a double shift. I couldn't get used to not being at work. One morning I got up early, as I'd always done, then headed off to work at Bolsover. I got as far as Arkwright, then I remembered, so I went into Chesterfield for a cup of tea in a cafe.

"Without my job, it was a totally different way of life. I didn't know what to do with myself. I'd just wander around the house.

"Melvin, another ex-miner, encouraged me to volunteer at the Derbyshire Unemployed Workers' Centre. I enjoyed it, I made friends. It still brings it home, though, when you talk about it."

Eric Eaton, who originally worked at Newstead in Notts, recalls that one aspect of the new Wild West in industrial relations was management's pro-UDM practices. The Coal Board, very keen to boost production, offered ad-hoc contracts for work to be done at weekends. If you were selected to work on such contracts, which meant working overtime, you would be very well-paid.

Miners who had been on strike were often in desperate financial circumstances, with all their creditors demanding immediate repayment, so they were keen to secure such contract work. NUM members were often refused such opportunities, though. Some miners apparently joined the UDM just to secure contract work that supplemented their incomes. It is thought that some Notts miners were in both UDM and NUM, not because they liked the UDM, but because they had access to overtime only if they joined that organisation. The NUM by that time had been refused recognition at pits in Nottinghamshire, so its members did not have a union with which management would even talk, let alone negotiate. That put the UDM in a powerful position. Management at some Nottinghamshire pits ensured miners could only get and keep jobs if they were a member of that breakaway outfit.

We never referred to the UDM as a trade union because we knew that it was created in order to damage the NUM, not to defend its members.

Although the NUM had lost the 1984/5 strike, NUM branches had not lost the will to employ energetic tactics in protecting their interests. Miners at Ireland in North Derbyshire were angered to find that management had placed several former scabs there who had been made unwelcome at their original Yorkshire pits. Ireland NUM members saw this as a provocation because importing faceworkers into Ireland would reduce job opportunities for local miners and their families at a time when the workforce was being slashed. Even the men who had scabbed at Ireland in 1984/5 joined the one-day strike, but it failed to change management's position.

Our sacked members MacGregor's Law had seen more than 960 of our members dismissed for activities during the strike. A Committee of MPs had made recommendations designed to help win back some of those jobs, but so far as I could tell those recommendations were ignored by the NCB, who refused to negotiate with National Officials about reinstatement. Although some jobs were won back through negotiations by Area officials, by January 1986 we still had 496 members dismissed. Some of those had been sacked for alleged offences, then found not guilty by the courts, yet were not allowed to resume their jobs. In Derbyshire a great deal of work went into those negotiations, with some success. Some miners who were not reinstated by the Coal Board found work with private contractor Cementation, which was keen to set on experienced men because the company would then benefit by winning NCB contracts without the union objecting to work being outsourced. Everyone benefited in a difficult situation.

Internal NUM checks on solidarity MacGregor's Law, designed to browbeat and fracture the mining workforce, sowed suspicion in the minds of our members. I always thought that, considered from a national perspective, the strike was broken first in North Derbyshire, then other Areas followed. In Notts the strike had never really taken hold, but in Derbyshire the vote had initially been almost evenly split, before Area Council decided to call its members to support the strike.

Coal Board Area director Ken Moses, with his bullying tactics, followed by the national November 1984 bribe of a huge bonus for anyone returning to work, had vastly reduced the number of strikers. Afterwards, miners in other coalfields came to mistakenly believe that all Derbyshire miners had been scabs. This could cause problems for specialist workers, often based at NCB workshops, who were sent regularly to collieries across England, Wales and Scotland for short periods to undertake short-term specialised jobs. NUM loyalists from Derbyshire were sometimes treated with great suspicion when they visited pits in other coalfields. Other NUM members might refuse to work with the Derbyshire men until their history was known, so several ways were found of avoiding that unpleasantness and disruption. Derbyshire NUM members would carry newly-printed NUM membership cards or letters from branch officials certifying their loyalty, but sometimes more was required.

When John Lander, a specialist in roof supports for coal faces, was sent to Goldthorpe in South Yorkshire, he was questioned closely by a union branch official, then invited to sit in the canteen while the branch official checked him out by ringing the two Derbyshire Area officials whose numbers John had supplied. As both Area Secretary and Area Treasurer then vouched for his loyalty to the union, John was made welcome at Goldthorpe and allowed underground. On another occasion John was sent to Tower Colliery in South Wales, where branch official Tyrone O'Sullivan carried out very thorough checks. Once assured of John's loyalty to the union, Tyrone welcomed him, sorting out his accommodation too.

13 The Lamp Cabin Two

Loss of my education budget At one NEC meeting in the middle of our prolonged financial crisis, Arthur announced that he was cutting the gardening allowances of the elected Area officials. Somehow he had acquired the power to determine parts of their pay, as well as the level of their individual retirement pensions. It seemed to me that was part of the ongoing battle for power between Areas and National Office, because the union had never been fully integrated into one unified structure. Instead each Area was an entity in its own right, owning property and employing its own officials, creating competing power-bases. Arthur's announcement clearly angered the NEC, most of whom were Area officials. If Arthur was cutting their allowances (although they had plenty of other allowances left) then some of them were looking for retaliation. I forget who it was, but one full-time official quickly suggested that as we were in financial difficulties the national education budget should be cut to zero. It seemed clear to me, without the words being spoken, that the proposer felt that wrecking the education budget, a National Office function, would avenge Arthur's assault on their incomes. Although I was horrified, we officers could only address the NEC if invited to do so by the President. Arthur did not invite me to defend the value of the national education programme before the decision was taken, within the space of a few minutes, to remove my entire budget immediately.

I felt shattered by that decision, by the careless way in which it was made almost instantly, as well as by the lack of thought about its consequences. As I could not recall any dissenting voices, it seemed to me that nobody on the NEC valued the union's national education programme. They had just cynically allowed it to be destroyed as part of an internal power battle between some Area officials and Arthur Scargill. Despite my belief that the decision was hugely damaging to the union as well as to my work, the Minutes merely stated blandly that it was agreed no expenditure was to be incurred except to promote the efficient running of the union. It was and still is a mystery to me how you could run a union efficiently while abandoning an education programme that tied together learning and skills with the challenges facing the organisation and the coal industry at that time of crisis.

After the NEC meeting I urgently needed to know if I was supposed to cancel the next planned residential school, already booked at Northern College. It would not be fair to them to cancel our booking unless Arthur said it was absolutely necessary. As I understood he would be going away immediately after the NEC meeting, I had to catch hold of him to get a decision. Immediately after the meeting I went out into the corridor, where he was having a discussion with Mick McGahey, to ask what I should do about the existing Northern College bookings. He did not want to think about that just then, but I persisted, explaining how urgent it was. If I had walked away then, as he clearly wanted me to do, I could not rely on him to answer my question before he left the building. In those days before mobile phones, I was never able to contact the officials once they were out of the building. Clearly very irritated, Arthur said that any existing booking should go ahead, so I managed to run one more school before the funding was cut off.

How could I run any sort of NUM education programme without a budget? As well as our usual need for members who understood what was happening, and how to think issues through, we had a pressing new need. Because of the breakaway resulting in the formation of the UDM, we had many newly elected, often inexperienced, branch officials, especially in Notts and South Derbyshire. They were operating in very difficult conditions under MacGregor's Law, with management in Notts refusing to recognise the NUM, and so refusing to give them time or facilities with which to look after their members. Our new branch officials would need some basic training. Well, I knew two other people besides myself who could offer that: my ex-husband Trevor Cave and my partner Barry Johnson, as we were all experienced tutors on TUC shop steward training courses. I organised a series of weekend training sessions for Notts branch officials, taught by Barry and myself, at Ollerton Miners' Welfare in North Notts. As that was one of the few Welfares in the coalfield still under the control of NUM loyalists, they allowed us free use of their premises and even found money to provide some food in the middle of the day. One of our students was Paul Whetton, formerly a miner at Bevercotes, whose unfair dismissal had been notorious even by the abysmal standards of the Coal Board's Notts Area under Area Director Bert Wheeler. We rounded off that course with a weekend school at Wortley Hall, which somehow managed to offer us free accommodation in our difficult circumstances. Trevor helped us teach that weekend course. Barry, working for a college, had no chance of any time off to compensate for his many weekends of teaching for the NUM, and of course I had no budget to pay him either. We both simply took it for granted that he would do that important work enthusiastically because of his devotion to the labour movement. Our South Derbyshire NUM Area, vastly reduced by defections to the breakaway UDM, had similar needs for branch officer training, so I borrowed the T&G union offices in Derby, then I taught a series of weekend sessions for them there. As we required a longer-term solution to our branch official training problem I approached the TUC, whose course development unit worked to create a version of Union Reps' training courses tailored for NUM branch officers. Because of Barry Johnson's detailed knowledge of the NUM, the TUC used him as consultant during that process. As our union was TUC-affiliated the courses were offered to us free of charge.

Weekend in Whitley Bay Sometime after the end of the strike I was asked by Northumberland Area to organise and teach a weekend school for them in Whitley Bay. As we sat round the dinner table on the first evening I noticed how much these Northumberland miners enjoyed a joke. As their accents were very hard for me to understand it took me a long time to grasp each joke, so I started to laugh long after everyone else. The school seemed to be going well. I had ended the evening session by giving them my standard Big Sister/Mother Hen speech, reminding them that the union was paying for them, so I expected them to turn up for the first session on Sunday morning in good enough shape to take an active part. Of course, everyone planned on going out that evening, as Whitley Bay was the pleasure capital of the North East. After the evening meal I was approached by a little group of the miners, inviting me to join them.

"Thanks very much, but I don't want to be out late. I'm teaching the first session in the morning. Anyway, I'm not used to places with lots of loud music." I was also aware that I didn't have any going-out-in-the-evening clothes. In fact my stock of clothes by then was well-worn with my low salary, loss of bonus during the strike and the Coal Board's delaying tactics in settling the NUM's outstanding pay claim. Our pay, related to what the miners earned, would not be increased until after the Coal Board deigned to settle the miners' pay claim that had been outstanding for well over a year.

"Howay, we can find some places you'll like, can't we, lads?"

So off we went an hour later. The keen wind felt as if it had come all the way from Norway, but these north-easterners barely seemed to notice. Hitching up my collar I decided that once I'd moved from Teesside to work in the balmy southern climes of Sheffield I must have grown soft. As we walked through the streets of Whitley Bay, I was surprised to count five, – yes five – bouncers outside each pub or club. We stopped off at a quiet hotel bar full of middle-aged couples having the occasional waltz. Even there we had to pass a full posse of doormen. The lads soon grew bored with the staid hotel, so moved on to a bar with few seats and lots of loud music. Just up my street, I thought wryly as we were about to settle in for the first drink – except that there was nowhere to settle. Instead we stood against small high tables, some built around pillars. After a while, as I wasn't going to let the men monopolize the round-buying, I insisted on buying a round. Waiting to be served at the bar I could see that the staff, both women and men, were wearing skimpy swimsuits or trunks. Just as I was trying to adjust to this sight, some hidden signal made them stop serving and begin to dance. The floor behind the bar was raised so the customers could see most of their bodies. Only by standing at the bar could you see the contrast between those glamorous upper bodies and what was normally hidden by the counter. All the dancers had rough training socks collapsing around their ankles, with heavy trainers on their feet. Was this a protest against the swimwear, or just a survival technique for busy Saturday nights? Finally I said goodbye to the lads, who were heading to yet another bar, and started walking back to the hotel. One of the group caught up with me.

"I thought I might walk you back to the hotel."

"Thanks, but I'm used to finding my own way home."

"I'd rather see you safely back."

Somehow I felt a bit uncomfortable. Was this a variation on "Save the Last Waltz for Me"?

"Well, it's kind of you, but there's really no need."

Feeling the need to hammer home my point, I added

"It doesn't mean anything. All we're doing is walking back to the hotel." I didn't want him nursing any illusions.

"Aye, all right."

Once we'd arrived inside the hotel, I thought it might be a good idea to sit down and talk to the others before going upstairs. Soon, though, I was ready for bed.

"Well, I'm off now. See you all in the morning. Goodnight." Gathering my coat and bag, I caught sight of the look of disbelief and annoyance on his face. So he had been nursing illusions after all.

Miners United Campaign After the strike ended Roger Windsor suggested that we needed a Miners' United campaign to remind our members, battered and fractured by our recent battles, of views we all shared. Thatcher's Law was forcing all unions to organise a ballot about our Political Funds, so I had already begun to prepare materials for that campaign. This was fairly easy to do because the TUC had provided excellent templates that could then be adapted by individual unions. Our NUM Political Fund Ballot Campaign was launched in Sheffield during the Annual Conference in 1985, with the ballot itself being held in December. I was relieved by praise from the specialist TUC worker for my adapted materials. The Tory Government, by forcing those ballots onto the trade union movement, had intended to damage the Labour Party, but all unions followed TUC recommendations by campaigning in a more general way about the danger of losing a voice in politics and Parliament, rather than focusing solely on the Labour Party. The TUC proposed a low-key workplace-based campaign rather than a high profile in the press that would have given Tories and newspaper proprietors the chance to shout down our arguments. That turned out to be the correct tactic, as every union won its ballot to "keep our voice". Our NUM ballot result was one of the best, delighting us all, so I was pleased to have been able to play a key role in one of our few victories over that period.

Roger called me to a meeting with himself and Trevor Cave, who was in charge of our relations with the Labour Party, to plan the rest of the Miners United campaign. We identified two additional topics which would help to unify our membership. Peace and Anti Apartheid were causes to which the NUM was already committed, as affiliated members of CND and the Anti Apartheid Movement. My share of that work included writing the booklet about Peace, challenging both Cold War divisions and the dangers posed by nuclear weapons. Borrowing some content from CND publications, I then supplied a draft copy to Peter Heathfield. When I saw him to check that he approved it, he said:

"I've had a quick scan through it, and I'm sure it's fine."

Worried by the toxic atmosphere within the union, I pressed him further.

"Would you mind reading through it very carefully, Peter, to make sure that there's nothing in there the right wing might object to. If someone complains you might end up having to defend it."

I could almost feel him suppressing a sigh as he thought of his busy schedule, but Peter was always supportive, so he agreed. When I next checked with him, he assured me

"I've read every word and I'm perfectly happy with it."

So I organised the print run and distribution. So far as I knew, no-one objected to any of the booklet's content. Reading it today I am struck by how relevant most of its points still are.

For the Anti Apartheid campaign I adapted a CND slogan to read "Together we can end Apartheid". Hunting for an image of two miners, one black, one white, for a poster, I rang the Yorkshire Area Office. Someone suggested that most pits did not have black workers because it was thought to be unspoken Coal Board policy to concentrate black workers into just a few pits. I was referred to the NUM Branch Secretary at Bentley, near Doncaster. When I rang him and explained what I was trying to do, he offered more than I had hoped for.

"I can find you two of our lads, one black, one white, who are genuinely best mates. Would that do?"

"That's brilliant, thanks, just what we need. Once you've asked if they're willing, just let me know when I can send the photographer round."

I still treasure that poster, with a copy on my wall at home.

Resuming the programme of national schools When at last my education budget was restored I was able to resume a programme of national residential schools, where we would socialise in the evenings. Occasionally I picked up mildly racist comments from some of our members so, feeling the need to tackle that, I organised a school called The NUM and the International Community. It focused particularly on South Africa and Apartheid, linking with one of our Miners United campaign themes. I agreed with Northern College that one of their tutors, who was Black, would address our first session to provide background information about Africa.

When he walked into the room, carrying neither notes nor images to show to the group, I feared the session would turn out badly. Most if not all of our students had never heard a Black person speaking as an authority on any subject. Despite my fears, this tutor held them spellbound, telling them about the university in Timbuktu that had existed at a time when Europe was in its so-called Dark Ages. I had also managed to secure as tutors both the London representative of the South West Africa People's Liberation Organisation (SWAPO) and the leader of the South Africa Congress of Trades Unions (COSATU) as speakers. The course seemed to have a profound effect on our students' understanding and attitudes.

We had huge and continuing difficulties, though, in the coalfields. Our members were being bullied, our union was being denied recognition in some coalfields, new and less safe working practices were being introduced and financial screws on the industry were being turned ever tighter. In October 1986 I ran a National School on Union Busting, working with Mick Clapham, who was head of our Industrial Relations team. Although it was valuable in helping us to understand the situation, such a school could not wrest power away from the Coal Board, which was operating as a bulldozer, crushing everything in its path.

14 The breakaway process

Over an extended period the new leaders in Notts had been distancing themselves from the rest of the union, changing their Rulebook so that it took precedence over that of the National NUM. No union would have tolerated that. By the summer of 1985, both Roy Lynk and David Prendergast, full-time officials in Notts, were undergoing disciplinary procedures because they had been acting against the interest of our union. A sub-committee of the NEC had been convened to examine their actions. To ensure objectivity, it met without the presence of National Officials. That group recommended that Lynk be dismissed and Prendergast be reprimanded. These recommendations were placed before a special meeting of National Conference delegates in Sheffield City Hall, where each man was given the opportunity to address Conference. To my surprise, Prendergast's speech was even more offensive than Lynk's. As he was finishing I could see several delegates almost lifting themselves out of their seats as they waved their arms to seek the President's permission to speak. Ken Capstick won that contest. Clearly sickened by the venom that had spewed out of Prendergast's mouth, Ken urged Conference to dismiss, not just reprimand, him. Others made the same demand, so it was agreed that both would be dismissed from the service of the NUM.

Over a period of months the new Notts Area leadership sacked the original Area Secretary Henry Richardson, his secretary Pam Elliott and Area president Ray Chadburn, who were all accommodated at National Office while they continued to work for the Notts NUM. All loyalists to the NUM in Notts had been hounded out of their Area office at Berry Hill, so what was called the Notts Miners' Forum, with delegates from every possible unit, met regularly on Saturday mornings. They were obliged to borrow the magnificent oak-furnished Area Council Chamber of Derbyshire Miners' Offices in Chesterfield. I attended those meetings because Arthur had asked me to take part in the unity campaign in Notts.

The new Notts Area leaders were preparing to formalise their breakaway from the NUM. Because they were arranging a ballot on the issue, we were organising rallies across that coalfield, urging members to vote to stay within the national union. We understood how impossible it would be to defend our members' interests if any sort of breakaway organisation were to be created.

With that ballot looming, a tiny sub-committee, including Mal Howarth of Blidworth colliery and myself, was set up to support the campaign against breakaway. Mal and I were trying to identify a slogan that would persuade Notts miners not to break away. We were standing in an aisle between the light oak pews, stretching our legs and backs after the long Forum meeting, trying out potential slogans. I can't remember who first said "Keep Notts National", but instantly we both knew we had hit on just the wording we needed. The stickers and badges created for the campaign were printed in green to represent Sherwood Forest.

Campaign meetings against the breakaway 1985 Over the next few weeks I helped out with the campaign, which included a number of meetings across the Notts coalfield. I recall one held in the Hucknall Sports Centre, with Ann Lilburn, then leader of the national Women Against Pit Closures movement, in the chair. Barry Johnson, vice-chair of the regional TUC, spoke on its behalf in his home town, with Arthur Scargill speaking for the NUM. I organised the main rally of our unity campaign at Mansfield Leisure Centre one Saturday afternoon. Arriving there in good time, I found our National Office receptionist Marilyn had turned up, but as she had a disability she could not climb the steps leading to the seats. When I asked one of the strongest-looking stewards if he could help her he assessed the seating arrangement, looked carefully at Marilyn, then picked her up gently and simply carried her to one of the highest seats in the hall, giving her a brilliant view of the stage. She was delighted. Once the meeting began I thought everything was going well until I was approached by a plain-clothes police officer, probably from Special Branch, who looked very serious.

"I need to inform you we've had a phone call saying there's a bomb in the building."

I felt a sort of lurch in the stomach, then began to suspect what was really happening.

"Do you think it's a genuine threat, or just a hoax?" I asked. I had read that the IRA had certain codes they used when alerting the police to bombs they had planted, so the police would know they were not hoaxers.

"Well, there are none of the identifying markers we would expect if it were a real bomb threat."

"So on balance you don't really think it's a genuine threat?"

"Probably not, but we can't be absolutely sure, and it's your decision whether or not to halt the meeting and clear the building."

"Well, I think the opposition are trying to force us to abandon our meeting by making the threat. I don't believe there really is a bomb, but I need to consult Peter Heathfield before I can give you a definite answer."

Now my problem would be to persuade Peter to talk to me while the meeting was continuing and while he was preparing himself mentally to give one of his powerful speeches. I tried to attract his attention without disturbing the current speaker, but understandably Peter didn't want to be disturbed at that moment, so brushed me off. I was forced to persist in a whisper.

"I'm really sorry Peter, but this is very urgent. The police say that there's been a bomb threat. They say there are no identifying markers that would prove it's a genuine threat, but they can't be sure. I think it's the opposition, trying to force us to abandon our meeting and wreck our campaign, so I don't think we should give them what they want. I can get the stewards to check discreetly under the seats for parcels, just to make sure. Do you agree that we should carry on with the meeting?"

He gave me a penetrating look, then agreed. No doubt Peter gave another of his excellent performances when he spoke that afternoon, but I was too busy to enjoy, or even notice, his speech. Pushing aside for a while my anger at the disgusting tricks the opposition were using, my next job was to talk to the stewards without creating a fuss that might alarm our audience. The last thing we needed was a panic. I managed to get the team together quietly in a little huddle, explained the situation then asked if they would try to look discreetly under the seats for unexplained packages. Finally I checked with them that they were happy with what I was asking them to do. Impressively, they all seemed determined to carry on calmly. As the others were moving away to start checking for parcels, John Evans of Duckmanton, who worked part-time as Peter's driver, came closer.

"Is there anything more you'd like me to do, Hilary?"

What better proof could there be of John's devotion to our union?

"If anything happens, make sure you look after Peter first – he's precious to us. Thanks a lot, John."

Along with the stewards, I kept looking at any space that could possibly hold a bomb. For the rest of the meeting I was hoping desperately that I had judged the situation correctly and that there was no bomb. If I turned out to be wrong, the consequences could be appalling and would be my responsibility, as I had led Peter into agreeing we should continue with the meeting. The event finished without any explosion, so it seemed clear that the breakaway merchants had simply been trying to frighten us into abandoning our meeting. I felt really pleased that we had called their bluff.

Yet our satisfaction did not last long, because the breakaway forces won the individual ballot of our Notts members. That was a tragedy for our members, seriously damaging our ability to look after their interests. Never called a trade union by the NUM, never recognised by the TUC as a genuine union, the organisation calling itself the Union of Democratic Mineworkers, or UDM, came into being. Initially we were told that it would be called the Democratic Union of Mineworkers, or DUM, but as our loyalists started calling its members Dummies, the name was suddenly adjusted. To nobody's surprise the UDM was eventually recognised as a union by the Tory Government-created Trade Union Certification Officer.

Many NUM loyalists in Nottinghamshire still refuse to utter its name, even forty years after its creation. Despite the right-wing national Labour Party leadership's hostility to the strike and to Scargill, the Labour Party never recognised the UDM either. That was partly because of the TUC stance, but more local influences were also brought to bear. I can remember hearing Barry Johnson ring his local MP Frank Haynes and explain in great detail why Frank should continue to support the NUM which sponsored him as an MP, and why he should argue within the Labour Party locally and nationally that they should never recognise the UDM as a genuine union with which they would work. Barry persuaded Frank, who was joined by other Labour Party figures in rejecting the UDM.

Proof that NCB management actively fostered the breakaway organisation came in a report to the November 1984 National Executive Committee by Jack Jones, general secretary of Leicester Area NUM. On the right wing of the Union for many years, Jack had made an impassioned speech to the National Executive early in the strike, complaining that National Office staff members were being used to further the strike. I had been surprised by his passion as he attacked what we staff members were doing: following the wishes of our managers the National Officials and giving support to the action our members were taking. Yet during the period when the breakaway organisation was being formed Jack Jones told the National Executive that senior Coal Board managers had tried to bribe him into taking his members into the UDM. They had promised he would not suffer financially if he did so. It might be worth looking again at that last sentence. How on earth could employers give such an assurance about the terms and conditions that would be offered to an official employed, not by them but by a trade union, unless that employer wielded great influence over, and was possibly funding, the emerging UDM? What was the point of a so-called union whose strings were being pulled by the employer? Although Jack would have seemed a likely candidate to graze the lush but toxic pastures of the UDM, with such favourable treatment guaranteed by Coal Board management, he did not leave us. That seemed to be because Arthur Scargill put in tremendous amounts of time and energy in persuading him to stay within the NUM, so we retained the bulk of the Leicester Area membership.

The formation of that breakaway organisation raised some difficult questions about trade union organisation. Neither the NUM nor any other TUC-affiliated union would sit down in a formal meeting with the UDM. Underground, though, the situation was more complex. If there was a problem with, perhaps, dust or water underground then miners would find the need to raise issues with management, or take direct action to tackle the problem. As neither dust not water distinguished between NUM and UDM members, miners on a particular coalface would sometimes take united action whichever organisation they belonged to. However, Arthur Scargill used his influence to squash any such unified action on the grounds that we did not talk to, or co-operate with, the UDM. I personally thought that unified action underground was a healthy, practical way of demonstrating the need for unity, a way that could lead to UDM members finally seeing the need for a single union, then rejoining the NUM. It seemed to me that such unified actions were very different from sitting down with UDM leaders in formal meetings, which would have meant that we recognised the UDM as a legitimate union. As a staff member, though, I held firm to the principle that it was for officials, our NEC and other decision-making bodies to make policy decisions, so I made no public comment about the issue, despite my own views.

15 Union woman

Zulu The only time one of our members treated me badly because I was a woman was during the first residential school I attended, which had been organised before I arrived and was really being led by the union's mining engineers. We were in a Sheffield University hall of residence, holding course sessions and socialising in the same large room, which I found a bit claustrophobic. During one evening, when the bar had been open for some time, one of the South Wales miners said something to me about doing a Zulu. I never fully understood whether this was part of rugby culture or South Wales miners' culture, but I knew enough to understand he was suggesting I should strip for their entertainment. What an insult! I was angry.

"Go to hell, Gareth!"

Suddenly the entire room was silent. I never knew if they'd heard what Gareth had said, but they certainly seemed to have heard my response. If I'd been a man Gareth would have hit me for that reply, but then if I'd been a man he wouldn't have suggested I should take my clothes off. Suddenly I noticed Des Dutfield from South Wales was standing next to me. With a little smile he said quietly

"She's right, you know, Gareth."

After a pause that seemed to last a very long time Gareth relaxed and the whole thing was over. I have always felt grateful to Des for that.

Encounter with Roy Lynk Arriving at the Nottinghamshire NUM Area Office in Mansfield felt a bit like arriving at a military encampment wearing enemy uniform. When I introduced myself the receptionist, a man, glared and puckered his nose as though the drains had started to stink.

"You're to wait there till Mr Lynk sends for you".

I sat down, contemplating the undoubted unpleasantness that was to come. I was only there because Pam Elliott, PA to the Notts General Secretary, had asked me to be her representative at a disciplinary hearing. An NUM loyalist, as was her boss Henry Richardson, her face no longer fitted once power in Nottingham Area NUM had been captured by the anti-strike, anti -national leadership faction led by Roy Lynk, one of the full-time officials. Accused of some trumped-up offence, she was to be hauled before the new Executive.

"I just don't trust my union rep – I think he's working with Lynk and co, so I want you to be my rep, if you're willing", she had told me on the phone.

So here I was, being ushered grudgingly into the Executive meeting room, with no real chance of speaking to Pam first.

Just before the door shut behind us, another figure slid inside.

"Who's that?" I muttered.

"That's my union rep" she murmured.

"Did you tell him when the hearing was?"

"No, because I didn't want him here – I don't trust him – that's why I wanted you to represent me. Management must have told him the date and time."

This quiet exchange was going on between us as we moved to our allotted seats. We continued to ignore her union rep, which meant all he could do was stand at the back of the room. Meanwhile, we were fully occupied. Roy Lynk let us know immediately that he intended to dominate this hearing, although in theory Area president Ray Chadburn was in the chair. Lynk, a large man who acted like a swaggering bully whenever I saw him, wasted no time in pleasantries.

"Who's this?" he demanded loudly, glaring at me.

I introduced myself as Pam's union rep.

"That's her union rep at the back of the room" he said, pointing at the man Pam did not trust.

"I'm a lay officer of our staff union Apex, I work at National Office, and Pam has asked me to represent her today".

It was as though a firework had erupted inside him: from his mouth exploded a stream of abuse. How dare I, one of Scargill's rubbing rags, come into Notts claiming to represent one of their staff members. Scargill was trying to interfere in the workings of the Notts NUM and he, Roy Lynk, wasn't going to allow that to happen. Who did I think I was? Did Scargill think they were stupid? As he shouted nastily across the large room, he was so agitated that his ample behind kept bouncing up and down on the seat. In a less fraught situation I would have burst out laughing. He ended by telling me to clear off, back to Scargill.

Arthur Scargill, of course, had no idea where I was, as I had cleared my absence on union duties with Peter Heathfield, who oversaw my work. There was no point, though, in mentioning this to Lynk, who never let a bit of truth get in the way of his prejudices. Anyway, I felt no need to justify myself to him. I had no option but to refuse Lynk's instruction:

"I'm not going anywhere – I came here to represent Pam".

"Get back to Sheffield, where you belong!"

"Pam wants me to represent her at this hearing, so I'm staying".

By now he was yelling rather than speaking, while still bouncing up and down. It was obvious that he was trying to intimidate me into leaving. As we continued to argue it out, Lynk shouting while I spoke calmly, I told him I would only leave if Pam wanted me to. After all, she was entitled to pick her own union rep at the hearing. Finally, Pam gave in and asked me to leave, as it was clear that the hearing wouldn't even begin until I did so. As I left, all I could do was to hope silently that she would survive this mauling without breaking down, alone in a room with the bullying Lynk and the hostile men of the new Notts Area Executive. Meanwhile, fuming silently about Lynk's behaviour, I tried to make a calm and dignified exit from the room. After all, I was only leaving because Pam had asked me to go. Walking out of the building I made a point of not noticing the receptionist's knowing smirk.

In due course Pam was dismissed by Nottinghamshire Area, along with their elected general secretary Henry Richardson. They were then given office facilities at National Office so they could continue to work on behalf of our members in Nottinghamshire. When Pam and I were talking about this incident many years later, she recalled

"The more Lynk shouted, the more quietly you spoke. I was very impressed by the way you handled it."

For years I had felt guilty about my unsuccessful attempt to represent Pam. After that discussion I could at least comfort myself with the thought that she had appreciated my efforts. When I checked the official Minutes of that meeting, I found an entirely different account of what had happened, an account that neither of us could match with our recollections. We trusted our memories, which were almost identical, rather than the official record.

A tale for snap-time: Billy's bag Bill Etherington, elected General Secretary of the Durham Mechanics' Area of our union, became an NEC member after the strike. Somehow people's names in the NUM always seemed to have a little flourish added by others, so Bill Etherington was known to everyone else as Billy. Highly committed to the union, Billy always seemed very serious, dressing more formally and traditionally than you might expect from a man of his age. As staff and NEC members were sitting in the meeting room one morning, waiting for the meeting to start, Billy walked in. I was startled by what he was carrying – it couldn't possibly be a man's handbag, could it? Today no-one would think twice about such a thing, but at that time it was considered very advanced, perhaps effeminate. As he walked around the meeting table to his usual place the room fell silent, every eye watching him in wonder. Billy was absolutely the last NEC member you might have expected to carry such an item. He said nothing but across the hush we could feel his powerful message: don't anyone dare say a word about my bag. When Billy reached his seat he placed the bag carefully on the table in front of him while the startled silence remained.

Working for the NUM We were often unhappy with the way the NUM treated us as employees. When I opened my first salary slip I spotted that, although my employment was supposed to have begun on May 1st 1983, I had only been paid from May 3rd. I went to Finance section to ask for the mistake to be put right but was surprised when they told me that Arthur Scargill had instructed them not to pay me until the 3rd, as the 1st was a Sunday and the 2nd was the May Day Bank Holiday. I think Arthur would have had something harsh to say to Coal Board management had they treated one of his members in that way. I never did receive pay for those first two days.

Before National Office was moved from London up to Sheffield most employees had opted for redundancy rather than a move up north. Arthur Scargill had taken that opportunity to downgrade the terms and conditions of employment of National Office staff. After that, employees paid more money into the Superannuation Fund but received less pension than before. He also decided that National Office staff would receive no overtime pay, however many hours they put in. Nationally negotiated pay was so poor that at least some Areas seemed to pay their staff more than we received at National Office. During the strike our APEX branch leadership had not pressed our own union demands on the NUM, but instead concentrated all our energies on trying to save the industry. Once that had been achieved there would be time to sort out our own issues – or so we had thought. We had also believed that our total commitment, including for some of us a year of regular unpaid overtime alone throughout the night in the Control Room, would be recognised and appreciated. It seemed we had been mistaken, as sometimes we were unable to obtain even basic trade union facilities from Arthur, who was in charge of staff relations, or HR, as it would be called today. After the end of the strike we wanted Anna, our APEX branch secretary, to access a TUC training course for lay workplace union reps. It would have meant her attendance at a college one day a week for a term, but for several months Arthur refused to agree to her absence. Around that time I wrote an APEX members' newsletter outlining all our staff union branch issues. I was delighted when Maurice Jones, editor of *The Miner* and a professional journalist, told me how good he thought it was.

My personal situation as an NUM employee was complex. I was solely responsible for education, but was not graded as a head of department, a situation I had accepted when I applied for the job. Some time after I started, but before Peter Heathfield took up his post as General Secretary, Arthur had told me that if they liked my work, I would be made a head of department after the strike. The National Officials seemed to like my work, so some time after the strike I went to see Peter to tell him about that past promise. He said that he would discuss the matter with Arthur and speak to me again. When we next met, I was startled and upset to hear that Arthur had denied that the promise Shad ever been made.

"But Peter, that would make me either a liar or a fool. I know I'm not a liar, and I don't think I'm a fool."

Peter looked uncomfortable, but I understood that he was powerless to do anything. We had known each other for years, so hopefully he knew me as an honest person. I understood, though, that he could never have accused Arthur of not telling the truth, based only on what someone else had claimed. That was the end of my hope of promotion at the NUM.

Negotiating with Arthur Scargill and Peter Heathfield Following major surgery I had been given a sick note certifying me unfit for work for three months. Feeling much better before the end of that period, I had returned to work informally, working just in the mornings, then resting in the afternoons. That meant I could set up arrangements for a series of campaign workshops in each NUM Area. At the end of the month I realised that my daily travel allowance, supposed to be part of my salary package, had not been paid. Staff in Finance said that withholding my travel allowance had not been their decision, so I went to our Chief Executive Roger Windsor. He claimed that Arthur Scargill had said I should not receive my allowance because I was only working half of each day. As it cost me just as much to travel to Sheffield to do half a day's work, I was angry, as well as short of money. By then I had set up arrangements for the workshops, so I decided to go home and rest for the remaining weeks of my certified sick leave. I stepped into the lift but just before the doors closed Arthur Scargill and his driver Jim walked in too.

"I'm going home!" I said.

He seemed surprised by my angry tone, which was quite different from my normal behaviour.

"Well, sometimes I feel like that, too."

I tried to explain.

"I've been coming in to sort out the arrangements for some workshops in the Areas, even though I'm officially certified as too sick to work, and now I find that my travel allowance has been withheld because I've only been working half days."

"Well, that would be Roger's decision, not mine."

This was getting worse.

"But Roger's just told me that it was your decision, not his, so who am I supposed to believe?"

I went home and rested until my sick note had expired. I was the chairperson of our APEX staff union branch, so as soon as I returned to work I spoke to our vice-chair Mick Clapham. We agreed to seek a union negotiating meeting with Arthur and Peter to request payment of my travel allowance. Of course we would have done the same for any of our members in my situation. When we met the National Officials we pointed out that I had been at work and spent money travelling there even though still officially certified as sick. Arthur refused to reinstate my allowance, claiming that it wasn't merited because I had only been working half days. So much for his claim that withholding the allowance had been Roger's decision. Peter, clearly embarrassed, offered to pay me out of his own pocket. To my surprise I burst out

"I'd rather die!" and found myself in tears, which was highly unusual for me, particularly at work. I knew that Peter was a kind and honourable man, acting with the best of intentions, but to be refused my entitlement, then offered charity instead, was unbearable. Peter was powerless to instruct finance staff to pay my travel allowance because Arthur had ensured that he himself was in charge of all staff matters. Our negotiation had failed. As we walked down the corridor, away from Arthur's office, Mick could sense that I was still very upset. Today I would have known that what I needed was a friendly hug from a colleague, but in the 1980's friendly hugs between colleagues were much rarer events than they are today. Unable to understand what I needed, so unable to ask for it, I settled instead for Mick's offer to take me to the kitchen and make me a cup of tea.

A tale for snap-time: The make-up session Arthur's driver Jim Parker had to spend many hours hanging around waiting to do his job, so we grew to know and like him. Although he also acted as Arthur's bodyguard he never seemed macho, but would join in the kitchen chat when we gathered at break-times. One lunchtime, following a National Executive

Committee meeting, as he waited to drive Mick McGahey back to the airport, some of the young secretaries decided to make up Jim's face. As he was happy enough to pass the time in this way they plastered on eye shadow, mascara and lipstick with lots of laughter and jokes. Unexpectedly Mick McGahey appeared in the doorway. Mick loved jovial company and talk, preferably in a bar, but it was clear that this was one joke he did not appreciate. I admired his self-discipline, though: although his face registered surprise, disbelief, then strong disapproval, he stayed silent. In the embarrassed hush, Jim hurried off to wash his face.

Negotiating with the NUM Delegation to the TUC Normally Roger Windsor and Trevor Cave attended TUC and Labour Party Conferences as delegates, sorting out the conference papers, liaising over compositing and generally running around making the elected officials' lives easier. In 1986 Yorkshire Area sent a letter to the NEC urging that in future only elected officials, not staff members, should be delegates to Congress. This was agreed by the NEC. Unaware of both the letter and the NEC decision, I was surprised by their results: Roger was instructed by Arthur Scargill to remain in Sheffield. Following hospital treatment, Trevor was off work sick, so he could not have attended anyway. Mick Clapham, our Head of Industrial Relations, came to my office one day during that TUC Conference, saying there was trouble. Scargill had rung Mick and told him he should travel down to Brighton to meet the NUM delegation, because some of them wanted to dismiss Roger Windsor for being absent from the TUC. Mick had pointed out to Scargill that I was the chairperson of APEX, our staff union branch, so I was the one who should be contacted. Scargill then suggested both Mick, as vice-chair, and I should go down to meet the delegation, with the NUM paying our fares and accommodation.

The irony of our situation struck us both. Our employers were inviting us down and promising to pay our travel expenses so we could defend one of our members against an attack from some of them. However, I at least could not have afforded to get on the train for Brighton unless someone else was paying the fare. The bonus element of our salaries, dependent on coal production, had stopped during the strike. As a single woman I had no financial buffer against this lack of cash.

It would have been no good asking APEX, our own union, for travel expenses in order to try to save the job of one of our members. We seemed to have an unspoken agreement with APEX that we would ignore them and they would ignore us. Although we were always careful to observe union rules in running our branch, we knew that the official APEX position had been opposition to the 1984-5 strike. Yet we, as NUM National Office staff, had all done whatever we could to carry out the wishes of the NUM membership in trying to make the strike a success. I knew of no staff member at National Office who had not been an enthusiastic supporter of the strike. Some of our staff had relatives who had been on strike, so they knew the hardships of no hot baths, shortage of food and cold homes. Although we knew we needed to organise ourselves into a union that was independent of the NUM, in order to protect our position, none of us had any enthusiasm for APEX outside our solidarity within our own branch.

Once Mick and I knew about the threat to Roger's job, we had to take action. Neither Mick nor I had Roger Windsor on our list of favourite colleagues, but as trade unionists we could not allow one of our members to be dismissed for simply following instructions from the National President. So we called an emergency APEX branch meeting for 5pm that day. Of course our members all agreed to support Roger, once we had explained what was happening. Armed with the union branch decision, Mick and I set off on the long train journey to Brighton. Once there, we would have to face the delegation, made up mainly of Area officials and National Executive Committee members, in order to defend Roger and save his job.

Just before the meeting we double-checked with Arthur that Roger was indeed absent from Congress in line with his wishes. As soon as we met the delegation I felt both the strained atmosphere and the strangeness of our situation. It seemed odd that the National President was on our side, but some members of the delegation were clearly scalp-hunting. Some did not speak at all, so it was never clear to me what opinions they held. I explained to them that Roger was absent on instructions from the President, and that our APEX branch was giving Roger unanimous support. I had assumed Mick McGahey as Vice-president and Peter Heathfield as General Secretary would both be supporting Arthur Scargill and therefore supporting our case for Roger. After all, they had nicknamed themselves The Troika during the strike, pushing back against the media portrayal of the strike as being led and run by Arthur alone. They liked to portray themselves as a unified force.

However, to my surprise McGahey started to probe: "When did your union branch give support to Roger Windsor?"

McGahey would not have allowed Coal Board management to inquire into when his members had reached a decision to defend one of their own. I was determined that nor would we allow such intrusive questioning, so I felt obliged to confront him.

"It's not up to you as our employers to ask that sort of question. I assure you our union branch has given unanimous support to Roger, and we don't need to tell you any more than that."

"I want to know about this unanimous support you say you have. How did you get it in such a short time?"

By then Mick McGahey was starting to get under my skin. I forced myself to stay calm and polite. "I'm sorry but we're not answerable to you as our employers about how we take decisions. We're only answerable to our members."

After this sort of exchange had been going on for a while, Mick Clapham said wearily "Tell them, Hilary, otherwise we'll never be able to move on."

I wasn't sure by this time whether my fellow union official Mick was more irritated by McGahey or by me, but I felt unable to maintain my stance without his support. So I told them about our emergency APEX branch meeting at 5pm the previous day, with its unanimous vote to support Roger. Then we explained again that Roger was only absent from conference because he was following instructions from President Arthur Scargill. Once the delegation had grasped that point, their blood-lust faded and our job was done, as they could make no further move against Roger. There seemed to be an atmosphere of seething resentment, though, among some members of the delegation. I heard Idwal Morgan. leader of the Cokemen's Area, who was normally calm and friendly, muttering angrily

"That ginger bastard..."

Although Mick and I had done our duty as trade union officers by saving Roger Windsor's job, I had been puzzled by Arthur Scargill's behaviour and very badly disappointed by Mick McGahey's attitude. That was how things were after the strike: you may not have done anything wrong, but you could find yourself caught suddenly on the barbed wire of someone else's battlefield, even though you were unaware that hostilities had commenced. Presumably Arthur had explained to the delegation, well before we arrived, that he had not wanted Roger to attend Congress. If the National Executive had taken a decision to ensure staff could not be TUC delegates, why had they not realised what that would mean in practice? If members of the delegation were still looking to dismiss Roger after the explanation I assumed Scargill had given, did they simply not believe Scargill? Why was McGahey so hostile? The whole thing was peculiar. Although I never had enough information to reach a conclusion about the wider questions, McGahey's hectoring of me, while I was operating as an elected lay union official, rankled for a long time.

Leaving It seemed to me that, of the many blows struck by the government against our union, the most lethal was to seize control of our funds. National Office and a number of Areas were all subjected at various times to that treatment, with some regaining control of their funds before others. All sorts of resentments were created by those government actions, on top of internal NUM personality clashes and divisions over tactics. According to Professor Vic Allen, who had advised the left caucus on the NEC for years, that group simply ceased to meet because relationships between various parts of the leadership had broken down. Uneasy with the general atmosphere that had resulted, although staff colleagues at National Office were not responsible for that, I became restive. One of the fundamental problems was that I had never really recovered from the shock of watching our National Executive remove my entire education budget within a few minutes as a tactic in the internal conflicts and personality clashes that had been raging for some time. It seemed clear to me that the National Executive did not value education and training for its members.

Thanks to MacGregor's Law, industrial relations in the industry had been turned into a live battlefield, where our side was constantly outgunned by the enemy. Pits and units were being closed one after the other, while our those of our members who had survived the closures were operating, very lightly-armed, in a free-fire zone where the enemy seemed to have unlimited Government-provided heavy weapons and armour. Although my budget had been restored I knew that an education programme could not make progress against the onslaught our members were facing. Of course I was sad in many ways to be leaving the NUM, where my work had formed part of nationally-important events. I had come to know so many miners and had developed great admiration, respect and affection for them. In my personal life as a single woman, though, I badly needed to return to better-paid work. Added together, all those issues led me to look for another job. Peter Heathfield had helped by providing a very good reference. Before my last day I went to see him, thanking him for his support. His response was memorable: "I hope you'll be happier in your new job, Hilary, than in the atmosphere we've managed to create here."

In fact I had never thought Peter was responsible for the bad atmosphere at National Office, although I felt an urgent need to escape from it. On my last working day with the NUM, 29th April 1988, it was five years almost to the day since I had started work there. Following our office tradition, I organised a staff gathering in the pub at lunchtime. Once everyone else had gone, Jim and I lingered for a while, chatting. Although I expected the NUM to appoint another National Education Officer, that never seemed to happen. I had put my lamp back on charge in the lamp cabin, but no one ever picked it up again.

Afterword

Hilary Cave's recollections of the miners strike of the mid 1980's is a remarkable document that we at Manifesto Press were immediately keen to publish.

Forty years after the events she lived through and describes her account loses nothing of its freshness. Detailed – based on documents, the historical record and her own recollections as a scrupulous and well organised educator – and persuasive through its transparent honesty, it is distinguished not only by a deep human sympathy for the striking miners and their families but by her political insight.

She brings to her account of her colleagues and the main figures in the union a real appreciation of their qualities as they faced the challenges that inevitably arise when workers confront not just their employers but the full force of the state's coercive apparatus and its ideological reserves in the monopoly media, .

Against her partisanship and deep solidarity with the miners and their union she is not uncritical of the union leadership and is frank about the pressures which inevitably faced a woman working in a male dominated environment, today and especially those four decades ago.

The text is valuable not just for its detailed account of the many crisis points in the conduct of the strike but for the consistent sense of class and political consciousness that permeates her telling of the story. It provides new insights into the struggles within the mineworkers union between the most class and politically conscious elements and the corrupted right wing who collaborated with the employers, the state, bourgeois media, intelligence organisations and the police.

Beyond that it gives some insight into those elements in the leadership of the Communist Party that abandoned their sense of class solidarity along with their capitulation to wider aspects of the dominant ideology and which precipitated a sharp conflict with its members that led to crisis, dissolution and a painful rebirth.

It is an unusual book in that it combines strikingly clear reporting of critical events in which she was an active participant with a convincing rendering of the many human encounters she recalls.

Hilary Cave retains a close connection with many of the protagonists who appear in the book and in the editing process memories were refreshed, details verified and perceptions sharpened.

The book is a valuable addition to the Manifesto Press series work/class/unions which combines works which tackle the real life problems of the working class movement and the trade unions from the standpoint of class solidarity and working class internationalism along with history, theory and analysis.

Manifesto Press is a cooperative and works in a cooperative partnership with the *Morning Star* where a proportion of the revenues go to the paper.

We work closely with with Strike Map, Liberation, the Education for Tomorrow collective and the Communist Party and for more than a decade we have worked with a wide range of labour movement organisations and campaign groups to provide publishing, design, promotion and marketing services and welcome enquiries about new projects and partnerships.

Nick Wright
Chair, Manifesto Press Cooperative

Other Manifesto Press publications:

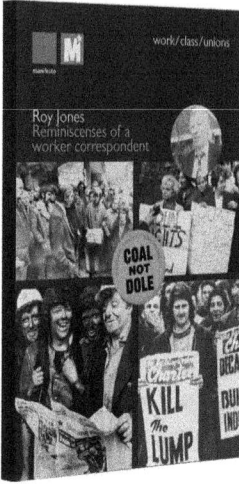

Roy Jones is the archetypical worker correspondent. From volunteer soccer reporter he became a well known and well loved industrial correspondent for the Morning Star. His Reminiscences of a worker correspondent trace his career fro itinerant construction worker blacklisted in sites throughout the country to a journalist who held the trust of workers and trade unionists in the dozens of strikes and disputes he covered.

He details the course of both the miners strike and other key disputes and the matches these against the developing crisis in the world communist movement and the British party.

Reminiscences of a worker correspondent
by **Roy Jones**

Mike Squires, author of the pioneering biography of Battersea Communist MP Shapurji Saklatvala returns to the tumultuous twenties to examine the roots of the Communist Party's Class against class stand in the fight against British imperialism, the party's solidarity work with colonial liberation movement particularly in India and the betrayals of social democracy.

Class against class deals with the bitter struggles of the period, charts the party's varying electoral fortunes and shows how the party built a strong base in factories, mines and working class communities and established the Daily Worker.

Class against class
by **Mike Squires**

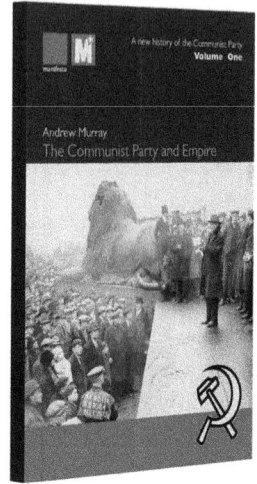

This first volume in Andrew Murray's new history The Communist Party and Empire deals with its formation in the politics of the turn of the century as British revolutionaries fought for working class power at the the heart of the world's most powerful imperialist state and at a period when proletarian revolution was a global reality and the prospect of a revolution in Britain haunted our bourgeoisie.

The book deals with the role of the Communist International, the roots in the betrayals of social democracy of the class against class strategy and sets the ground for future volumes.

The Communist Party and Empire
by **Andrew Murray**

Order on the Morning Star online shop:
shop.morningstaronline.co.uk

f **@Manifesto Press**
𝕏 **@Manifesto_Press**
⌾ **@manifestopresscoop**

f **@The Morning Star**
𝕏 **@M_Star_Online**
⌾ **@themorningstaronline**

Other Manifesto Press publications:

ROGER McKENZIE

AFRICAN UHURU

THE FIGHT FOR AFRICAN FREEDOM IN THE RISE OF THE GLOBAL SOUTH

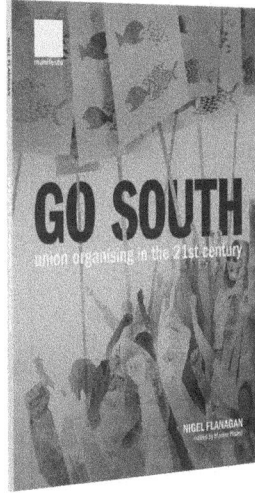

GO SOUTH
union organising in the 21st century

NIGEL FLANAGAN

The Eurocentric world is dying. The key question is how do we make its replacement in the interests of the people rather than the ruling class.

One of the key reasons for our arrival at this pivotal moment in history is the role that Africans on the continent and across the diaspora have played in developing revolutionary thought and action.

But where this contribution has not been completely ignored it has been barely recognised. This book charts the building of African communities of resistance in Britain as part of the fight against racism and the building of a new world.

African Uhuru
By **Roger McKenzie**

Are the trade unions back? After the strike wave of 2022 and 2023 the unions are in a better place – more relevant, more active and more popular. They have achieved much in the last 2 years for their members during the worst cost of living crisis since the war. But what next?

As strike days are falling again to pre 2022 levels and membership of trade unions is only showing qualified increases it seems that unions must look outside for inspiration. This books discusses where they might find it – in the Global South.

Go South
By **Nigel Flanagan**

Order on the Morning Star online shop:
shop.morningstaronline.co.uk

f @Manifesto Press
X @Manifesto_Press
○ @manifestopresscoop

f @The Morning Star
X @M_Star_Online
○ @themorningstaronline

Cover image

Hilary Cave recounts: "The picture, by NUM member Percy Riley, shows me speaking outside the 19 April 1984 Special Delegate Conference where the decision was taken to call all miners out on strike.

"Thousands of NUM members, following the union's tradition, were outside the conference, lobbying delegates to make the strike call. I organised the rally to keep our lobbyists occupied. The picture shows the very end of the rally, where I was telling the crowd where to find their buses, then advising them to resist anticipated provocations by the police."

Thousands join rallies to save coal indust

Midlands behind the mine

TH ONE VOICE, tens of usands of trade unionists on y Day marches, demonstrations l festivals across the East and st Midlands at the weekend lged their full support in secur- victory to the miners.

In dozens of speeches, on usands of posters the message s the same: Victory for the iers is victory for all working ple. Defeat for the miners is eat for us all.

Teachers, local a u t h o r i t y rkers, school dinner staff, un- ployed youth, pensioners — every

section of workers in struggle now see the miners' cause as their own.

Nothing could make this more clear than the way miners pickets from Wales, Yorkshire, Notting- ham, Derby and Staffordshire were given an honoured place in the ranks.

The turnout at the demonstra- tions, the biggest-ever in some places, ranged from 300 in Telford to 10,000 in Chesterfield. Thousands more marched with banners and bands in Mansfield, Nottingham, Stoke-on-Trent, B i r m i n g h a m, Derby, Leicester and in dozens more Midland towns.

Notts pits urged: join strike wave

By JIM SAUNDERS

NERS' union leaders yes- lay appealed to Notting- ishire miners who are still

"Support from the rail unions has been magnificent," he sail. "But we can't expect their members to be sent home when we've still got our members go-

cruise missile launcher, an ambu- lance and a fire engine also travelled on the march.

"The miners' strike is not only about jobs, but whether we are

With brass band playing and banners and heads held high, 10,000 trade marched through Chesterfield yesterday in one of several May Day marches out the weekend.

▲ Solidarity! The *Morning Star* front page with news report and picture of the May Day 1984 Chesterfield rally

Right: Hilary Cave recounts: "This is the Miners March on Mansfield, which I organised jointly with

Roger Windsor. I was arrested while driving him through north Nottinghamshire to meet the police and some Mansfield District Councillors, whom we believed were working miners, to negotiate its route. I had worked with Ida Hackett, leader of the Notts

Women's Support Groups, to accommodation for some pick who were willing to stay in the county to picket, instead of tr to pass police road-blocks on county boundaries. I later repo that 40,000 members and supporters had attended."

MINERS UNITED

TOGETHER WE CAN END APARTHEID

...eaking is president of Chesterfield Trades Council Barry Johnson, ...s left is Jack Taylor, Yorkshire NUM Area president; to his left, ...lon Butler, area secretary for North Derbyshire and Tony Benn, ...y elected Chesterfield MP and a great supporter of the miners.

▲ After the strike, a Miners United campaign was mounted. For the poster two miners, from Bentley colliery near Doncaster. were identified by their branch secretary because they were genuine best friends .

Milton Keynes UK
Ingram Content Group UK Ltd.
UKHW020707021224
3298UKWH00040B/430